So Spirited a Town

So Spirited a Town
Visions and Versions of Liverpool

Nicholas Murray

Liverpool University Press

First published 2007

Liverpool University Press
4 Cambridge Street
Liverpool L69 7ZU

British Library Cataloguing-in-Publication Data

A British Library CIP Record is available.

ISBN 978-1-84631-128-4

Set in ITC Giovanni by
Koinonia, Manchester
Printed in the European Union by
Biddles Ltd, King's Lynn

in memory of
W. G. Murray (1913–1997)

Contents

Preface

This is a book about Liverpool seen through the eyes of writers of the past. I have left the living their space to grow. It aims to build a picture of the city as it has been transmitted through the shaping imagination of writers, most of whom, though writing non-fiction rather than fiction, read and represent the city in new ways.

But this is also a book anchored by some memories of my own as someone born in Liverpool in the 1950s and growing up in a city in which my family has lived since at least the early nineteenth century.

My own memories – such are the creative tricks played by recollection, its sly re-orderings and outrageous inventions, its barefaced subjectivity – may turn out to be just as much works of the imagination as those of the novelists and poets I have assembled.

Liverpool is about to be celebrated as the European Capital of Culture. The debate will rage about what that notoriously slippery term 'culture' signifies. But one thing is clear: Liverpool remains a lively independent city with a distinctive culture all of its own.

My book is largely about versions of Liverpool's past, and how that past continues to exercise its influence on the present, and about my own childhood and adolescent years. I have not lived permanently in Liverpool since the 1970s and therefore this is not a book which makes a claim to be any sort of insider's guidebook to the city today. Plenty of such books exist and they are not my rivals.

More than this, I am sceptical of books which seek to define the 'true' or 'real' character of a city. Cities are complex entities, many-layered, wary of the levelling tyranny of the fashionable or 'cool', of the guide who claims, preposterously, to have his or her 'finger on the pulse' of the city. In a contrarian, fiercely individualistic city like Liverpool such an authorised version is a special kind of absurdity. Cities are open to multiple readings, charged with subtle ambiguities, polysemic, elusive, tantalising. That is why they excite us.

This book is dedicated to my fellow Liverpudlians, and to my family, who taught me to find life funny in the way that Liverpudlians do – or did in my youth; especially my father, whose 'Scouse humour' may not yet be entirely obsolete in a twenty-first-century European Capital of Culture and which I still recall with an affectionate chuckle.

I would also like to thank all those who have helped me to identify writers who have recorded their impressions of Liverpool and especially Gladys Mary Coles whose pioneering anthology *Both Sides of the River* first persuaded me to start my library-explorations. It has been an interesting journey. I owe very special thanks to Colin Lovelace, former assistant manager of the Liverpool Playhouse, for offering me a generous recollection of the theatre's mid-sixties' artistic ferment.

I

The Strange Dream of Doctor Jung

'Listen, mate!' said the fat man, the soft corpulence of his body spilling out over the double front seat of the bus like a heap of sand poured from a build-er's wheelbarrow.

His plump hand grasped the chromium bar beneath the upstairs window. He seemed to direct his words not towards his 'mate' but straight ahead at the moving picture of the city streets which unreeled through the window. He was dressed in what was once the unofficial uniform of the British working man: a cloth cap pushed back on the head, blue denim jeans, and a black donkey jacket. Where, I wondered idly, could he have found a pair of jeans big enough? The city centre army surplus stores where workman's clothing was sold could surely not have kept in stock anything in his size. The leather band across the shoulders of the donkey jacket advertised the fact that it was on the uncomplaining back of the stoic British prole that all burdens fell.

The fat man's mate was a comic contrast, Stan Laurel to his Oliver Hardy. His thin, elongated neck – stretched in the manner of a character in an animated cartoon – ended in

1

a wild shock of red hair. Much later I would come across Laurence Binyon's description of the poet Algernon Charles Swinburne: 'the long solid neck above sloping shoulders supporting a massive head and a fiery cloud of hair'. That was about right. Both men held their conversation without turning their heads. Fatman on the left of the aisle, Algernon on the right, their eyes never meeting. I was the only other passenger on the top deck of the red Ribble Bus Company service that was heading towards the centre of Liverpool from the northern suburbs. I was a student at the University and on my lap was the crimson paperback *Oxford Standard Authors* edition of the poet Edmund Spenser. The date was probably 1971. Fascinated as I was by the Elizabethan poet's rich and decorative imagination, it could not defend itself against the pull of the real world. I had stopped reading.

Looking at the two men I sensed something familiar. A few weeks earlier, coming back on another late-night bus, I had seen these seats occupied by two Chinese seamen. They, too, were conducting an unconnected conversation across an empty aisle, faces rigidly forward, speaking in a rapid, animated language that naturally was opaque to me. They wore shiny black leather jackets and, as the bus neared the entrance to the Gladstone Dock at Seaforth, they suddenly sprang up and clattered down the stairs. Under the weak glow of a street lamp I watched them go – still several feet apart, still jabbering – along the cobbled street back to their ship.

Fatman and Algernon had evidently been talking about their sense of belonging, vying with each other for the palm of being the truest *echt* Scouse.

> 'Listen, mate! My family have been in Liverpool since Julius Caesar paddled up the Mersey on a binlid.'

This finished off Spenser for good. It was textbook Liverpool

2

humour: the mock-aggression ('Listen, mate!') of people who wouldn't hurt a fly, the mad surrealism, the playfully affronted tone, the verbal dexterity, but – and this was the oddest thing – the strange absence of laughter. If this was a joke why weren't these people smiling? Why weren't the tears running down those cheeks I couldn't see?

And there was something else. Had I perhaps heard this crack before? Had the fat man? Oral culture has no authorship, no canonical texts, no formal citations. It lives a free, unconnected life. It has no copyright, no contracts, no premium on originality. Anyone can pick up a riff or a gag and run with it. Improve it. All that is required is that it shall work. At best one can add a phrase, a minor embellishment, to a formula as it passes in and out of one's mouth, off who knows where.

Fatman's quip reminded me of my single visit to a football match. Football is a Liverpool passion which I hardly dare admit I have never been able to share. The essential gene was missed at my making, but I considered that, just once, I should put myself on the terraces as an insurance against my future self-respect. I agreed to accompany a friend who was going to a match at Anfield between Liverpool and Leeds. On the notorious Kop – named after the Boer War battlefield of Spion Kop where a Liverpool regiment suffered heavy casualties – the crowd swayed backwards and forwards like an advancing and receding Atlantic roller. Halfway through the game a lean, wiry Leeds player called Billy Bremner got hold of the ball and began to race down the wing, showing every sign of preparing for a breach of the Liverpool defence. The Kop erupted in fury and concentrated all its hatred on the scanty figure of Bremner. A furious spectator behind me yelled at the top of his voice: 'I've seen more meat on a fly's lip!'

Julius Caesar did not, in the dull, humourless, real world, ever sail up the Mersey but the Romans settled across the

Wirral peninsula at Deva – modern Chester. Liverpool was considered then, and for most of the ensuing centuries until the eighteenth, a low-lying, swampy, unprepossessing place – the name Mersey deriving from its marshy banks. It was a very late developer as a port. Historians generally dismiss the pre-history of a city that was not even mentioned in the Domesday Book and whose early historical remains are vestigial. Liverpool took off in the eighteenth century, its fortunes built on the slave trade, and its pre-eminence as a port continued to increase throughout the nineteenth century.

During the English Civil War, Prince Rupert and his Royalist troops were camped on Beacon Hill, Everton. The Royalist commander looked down contemptuously on the Roundhead soldiers who were in possession of Liverpool Castle. The fortification, Rupert mocked, was 'a mere crow's nest which a parcel of boys might take'. Even as late as 1873, the French observer Hippolyte Taine still considered it 'less adapted for men than for wild duck'. But the city's great era coincided with the Victorian epoch, whatever a Gallic sceptic might think.

I was born in Liverpool in 1952 and grew up, it always seemed to me, in the living aftermath of the Victorian period. The cityscape was one of cobbles, cast-iron bollards, massive nineteenth-century wharves and warehouses and dock walls more formidable than those of a Venetian fortress in the Morea. I spent my childhood and adolescence in the northern suburb of Waterloo, many of whose streets were named after battles and generals of that conflict – Blucher Street, Waterloo Road, Wellington Street, Murat Street. This was well before the rise of urban chic, which took so long to reach Liverpool. It is only now that the gentrification of old terraces and restoration of early nineteenth-century warehouses, with the inevitable luxury flats and all the paraphernalia of the heritage industry, has enabled the city to catch up with other, more prosperous, cities in the post-industrial urban landscape stakes. And now it has received the accolade of European Capital of Culture. Not in the sense that the word would be understood by Matthew Arnold, who died here, but let's not be pedantic.

Mine is a risky inheritance, for the world does not always appreciate the Liverpudlian taste for facetious humour, its horrified recoil from *gravitas*. The bookshops and tourist information centres in the city are full of books with titles like *Lern Yerself Scouse*. These merge with anthologies of Scouse humour. A typical example of the latter – with that mixture again of mock-aggression and permitted insolence – would run like this:

> Woman to bus conductor: 'Does this bus stop at the Pier Head?'
> Bus conductor to woman: 'There'll be a bloody big splash if it doesn't, luv.'

This is not, it hardly needs saying, very sophisticated humour, but it is the joking of people who have tended to fashion their humour out of the bare materials to hand. It is the wise-cracking of a woman at a bus stop or a man in a spit-and-sawdust saloon bar who hasn't much to do but gag his way out of lean times: 'It's so rough round our way,' the comedian quips, 'we take in the doorsteps at night.'

The accounts of Liverpool by Nathaniel Hawthorne, who was American consul in the city, or Herman Melville, who described it in his novel *Redburn* in 1849, or Dickens, de Quincey, Francis Kilvert or Gerard Manley Hopkins, Karel Čapek or Nikos Kazantzakis, present an unrelenting picture. They insist on poverty, overcrowding, squalor – particularly among the desperate Irish immigrants whose ranks swelled in the wake of the Famine in the 1840s. Hawthorne wrote in his notebooks of the 'ragged Irish barefooted women' and the sensitive poet Hopkins hated every minute of his stay as curate in the slum parish of St Francis Xavier's (known to every Liverpudlian as 'SFX').

Everyone knows about the Liverpool Irish but – quite apart from its considerable Welsh population, who had far less distance to travel in order to get here – the Lancashire hinterland has always been a vital element in the formation of Liverpool's identity. Like the Vatican City in the heart of Rome, Liverpool and its cheeky Cockney vivacity sit as an island in the staider sea of Lancashire.

My own family roots lie in both the Liverpool Irish and the Lancastrian. My maternal grandfather, James McElroy, was for a quarter of a century Secretary of the Irish Club in Kirkdale and a prominent member of the Ancient Order of Hibernians. My great-great-great-grandfather, James Murray, came to Liverpool from County Mayo in the middle of the nineteenth century. But my paternal grandmother's family, the Howarths, came from the hamlet of Dinckley in the Ribble Valley. I don't know about Julius Caesar, but we have been in Liverpool and Lancashire for a very long time.

My sister always insists that she was born in Lancashire and I always say that I was born in Liverpool. It turns out that we are both right. Lancashire Education Committee looked after our schooling but we lived in a Liverpool postal district. One day a policeman came to our door in Waterloo after a mysterious suitcase was delivered to the house in error. He had a strong Lancashire accent and, because our house looked directly onto the seafront, he assumed that he was calling on the equivalent of the Morecambe or Blackpool seaside landladies he knew so well. 'Eee, I thought these were all boardin' 'ouses,' he said when we enlightened him. After he had left, bearing away the suitcase (whose true story we never

6

learned) we children fell about in laughter at this Lancashire bumpkin, repeating for the rest of the day in peals of mirth: 'Eee, I thought these were all boardin' 'ouses.'

I see now that this was harsh and unfeeling of us wretched kids, not least because of its unfair pillorying of the Lancashire folk. Later I would bridle at Melville's reference in *Redburn* to the unfortunate Lancashire boy who had failed to make good in America and who was now trying to work his passage home to Liverpool on the same boat as the writer: 'He talked such a curious language, though, half English and half gibberish, that I knew not what to make of him.' Scarcely less prejudicial was Daniel Defoe, who came to Liverpool in 1721 on his *Tour Through the Whole Island of Great Britain*. He expected to be met at the Mersey ferry by a small rowing boat or a horse. Instead he found that you were raised 'on the shoulders of some honest Lancashire clown, who comes to the boat side, to truss you up, and then runs away with you, as nimbly as you desire to ride'. Defoe, it should be pointed out, did go on to add that 'Liverpool is one of the wonders of Britain'.

These eighteenth- and nineteenth-century writers at least based their reports on experience. The most extraordinary account of Liverpool in the twentieth century, however, was by someone who never saw the city: Carl Gustav Jung. In his autobiography, *Memories, Dreams, Reflections*, published in 1963, the great psychologist recounted an odd dream. He found himself in 'a dirty, sooty city' – so far so good – through whose streets he walked in the company of a number of fellow Swiss. He had the sense in this dark dream that the city was up above on the cliffs. In his climb there from the harbour it came, in his dream-consciousness, to resemble Basel. In that town one climbs from the market place up to the plateau where the Petersplatz and the Peterskirche are located, through the grim-sounding Totengäschen (the Alley of the

Dead). Liverpool, too, rises from the waterfront at the famous Pier Head to the high ground of Everton Brow or Brownlow Hill. It was there, as late as the early 1970s, that I remember seeing an Orange march, a tiny survival of the old sectarian rivalries. These have long ago vanished from Liverpool, along with the riots during which Catholics lobbed half-bricks – 'Irish confetti' – at the Protestants. As a Catholic schoolboy in the 1950s I would think it quite natural to describe 'non-Catholics' (itself a revealing formulation) as 'Proddy-Dogs'.

When Jung had climbed through the darkness of his lugubrious dream to the plateau projected by his phantom Liverpool he found a broad square dimly illuminated by street lights, into which many streets converged. The different quarters of the city were arranged radially around the square and in the centre was a round pool. In the middle of the pool was a small island surrounded by an obscurity of 'rain, fog, smoke and dimly lit darkness'. The island itself blazed with sunlight. 'On it stood a single tree, a magnolia, in a shower of reddish blossoms. It was as though the tree stood in sunlight and was at the same time the source of light.' His companions spoke of another Swiss who was living in Liverpool and the dreaming Jung told himself that he knew very well why the man would choose to live near this glowing, restorative source. Then he woke.

Jung later analysed his dream, suggesting that it was a representation of 'my situation at the time'. The grimness, the darkness, the greyish-yellow raincoats glistening with rain, expressed his own sense of personal desolation. 'Everything was extremely unpleasant, black and opaque – just as I felt then.' His description of that illuminated tree makes me think of Christmas Eve in Liverpool when my father often took me to visit his poor relations in another part of the city and we passed through Clayton Square – now a boring shopping mall – where every year an enormous Norwegian Christmas tree blazed with light. It always seemed dull and foggy on these excursions, the child longing for the compensatory excitement of Christmas morning and its bulging stockings, the tree, for now, a bright beacon of expectation.

Jung's dream had offered him 'a vision of unearthly beauty, and that was why I was able to live at all'. He should have stopped his account there, with that healing vision of supernatural light. Instead, Jung demonstrated that he was an eminent psychologist but a hopeless etymologist. Liverpool, he said, summing up the meaning of the dream, is 'the pool of life' and the liver, according to ancient tradition, is the seat of life, that which, as he puts it, 'makes to live'. Alas, it signifies no such thing. 'Liverpool' refers to a 'low-lying' pool, hardly a source of rebirth and resplendent light, 'less adapted', to repeat the words of Taine, 'for men than for wild duck'.

But we Liverpudlians are grateful to Jung for the thought. There are worse ways of representing a city than as a pool of life. The claim no doubt is a little grand for our modest, self-mocking sense of our town. Civic pride of the grander variety we tend to leave to those better at that sort of thing – the Mancunians, for instance. A quip on the top deck of a bus. A sniff of the breeze coming off the Mersey. A chirpy 'All right, mate!' from one side of the street to another. These are more in our line. Liverpool's civic pride is not a matter of pomp and puffed-up satisfaction. It wears itself lightly and, I have always felt a little blasphemously, finds a poor echo in all those neo-classical columns and capitals on St George's Plateau.

Nevertheless, it is satisfying to know that Jung found solace and renewal in the mere thought of the place.

9

2

The Boy in the Playground

One morning in the late 1950s a door opened in one of the infant classrooms in St Peter and St Paul's Roman Catholic Primary School, Crosby, Liverpool 23. We all turned our heads expectantly to where the headmistress, Sister Rose, of the Convent of the Sacred Heart, stood with her hands resting lightly on the shoulders of a small, tousled boy in baggy grey shorts.

Headmistresses are meant to be fire-breathing dragons but Sister Rose was a very gentle nun. The narrow Gothic arch of her wimple kept one, as it was meant to do, at a distance. Inside it, like an Easter egg in its box, only part of her head was visible in a surround of tight, white material that excluded hair, ears and neck. But her soft cheeks, when she bent down to address one of her pupils, were suffused with a delicate pink blush. Even as a six-year-old 'infant' I was struck by the appropriateness of her chosen name, though I cannot recall why I was in her study, and why she was stooping to me, for I was never the sort of pupil who collects gold stars or comes top of the class, or, for that matter, commits the sort of misdemeanour that gets one carpeted.

My other memory of Sister Rose can be given a very precise date: 29 June 1959, the Saturday after the feast of Corpus Christi, when I made my first Holy Communion. She and her fellow nuns came round the open air trestle tables with plastic washing-up bowls filled with boiled eggs, doling them out to the boys with their white shirts and medals threaded with a blue ribbon, and the girls in their best frocks.

On that other morning, however, all eyes focused on the small boy whom Sister Rose now left in the teacher's care. Arriving like this, in the middle of term, in the middle of the morning, would have been amazing enough, but there was something else about the boy – who was introduced to us simply as 'Teddy' – that astonished us. From the top of his curly hair to the tips of his toes, Teddy was completely black! We had never seen such a thing, except in photographs or in the posters of the missionary priests who exhorted us to save our pennies for the 'Black Babies' appeal. In the north Liverpool suburb of Crosby in the 1950s the only experience we had of ethnic minorities (the term was not then in use) were the people at the Chinese laundry where I was sometimes sent to collect starched collars or tablecloths from a woman who stood to deal with orders at a tiny, rudimentary wooden hatch.

As soon as the bell rang for the first break everyone filed out into the tarmac playground behind the school. I wasn't among the first to reach the yard but when I finally got there another extraordinary sight met me. Teddy was running furiously across the yard, his tiny but powerful legs pumping up and down, his grey shorts fluttering in the breeze. Behind him, like the rippling tailfeathers of a kite, followed what looked like at least half the school. In a long, laughing line, they followed behind Teddy as he executed wide, sweeping loops and arabesques, the look on his face not a look of terror

11

or fear, rather one of determined seriousness. It was as if he expected this and that no other possibility existed. He simply kept on running. I did not join in the pursuit but I watched and was complicit. Round and round, up and down, little Teddy ran until the bell sounded again.

Perhaps he is running still.

'This is a story of an invisible people,' begins Ray Costello's history of Liverpool's black community, *Black Liverpool* (2001). With one of the oldest black communities in Britain and one of the oldest Chinese communities in Europe – not to mention the dozens of other ethnic communities who make up the population of a city Thomas de Quincey called in *Confessions of an English Opium Eater* 'many-languaged Liverpool' – the port ought to be seen as a model of multicultural richness and lively cosmopolitanism, but in the 1950s, especially in the outer suburbs, visible signs of that ethnic diversity were completely absent. Even now the 'invisible people' can still be missed on a walk through the city centre.

Liverpool's wealth was derived from the slave trade – a fact it has sometimes contrived to overlook – but that is not the reason why there is a very long-standing black presence in the city. A popular Liverpool myth was that the great iron chains in the Goree Piazzas (demolished after being bombed in the Second World War and formerly situated where The Strand is now, behind the Mersey Docks and Harbour Board offices) were used to tether slaves rather than (much more likely) carriage or draught horses. The slave trade – which we shall be looking at in a later chapter – was a triangular one, with the second of the three sides – the notorious 'middle passage' from West Africa to the plantations of the West Indies – happening well out of sight of the gentlemen in cocked hats who strolled up and down the Goree Piazzas. Once in a while a handful of slaves would be brought back to Liverpool and there is plenty of documentary evidence from the eighteenth century of small auctions of a handful of slaves at the coffee houses or on the Custom House steps, but as Ray Costello explains, 'One of the largest single contributions to the Liverpool Black population is that of black sailors settling in the port'. In addition, in the eighteenth century, sons of African chiefs were encouraged to come to England to be educated and to be persuaded of the charms of Empire. Some in Liverpool's black community have aristocratic blood. After the American War of Independence numbers of those black troops who had identified with Britain came and settled in Liverpool. The Elder Dempster Line hired many black sailors on its ships between Liverpool and West Africa, and some of these sailors settled in Liverpool, where they often intermarried. Pat O'Mara, author of the scarifying account of early-twentieth-century low-life Liverpool, *The Autobiography of a Liverpool Slummy* (1934), alleged that many Liverpool girls preferred black husbands because they were less addicted to drunken wife-beatings (and were often away for longer periods!). Similar claims have been made about Chinese husbands.

At least one prominent black Liverpudlian has a street in the city named after him. James Clarke was born in Jamaica in 1880 and stowed away at the age of 14 in a ship bound for Liverpool, where he was adopted by a family of Irish descent near the docks. He was a great swimmer, especially underwater, and earned a reputation for rescuing people from the Leeds–Liverpool canal. The police would frequently ask him to retrieve drowned bodies so that they would not have to run the risk of damaging them with their grappling hooks. Clarke was a popular member of the Vauxhall community that pressed for the street to be named in his honour.

Less happy was the experience of Charles Wootton. He was a young Bermudan seaman who became caught up in the 1919 race riots in Liverpool. These broke out after white workers at some of the city's oil mills and sugar refineries refused to work with their black workmates, whom the companies then promptly sacked. In May of that year individual blacks were attacked in the streets as well as in their homes and lodgings. Sometimes the racist mobs were 10,000 strong. Elder Dempster's hostel for black seamen and the David Lewis Hostel for black ratings were also attacked. Charles Wootton was chased by a large mob and stoned to death after leaping into George's Dock to save himself. It was alleged that the local police declined to intervene. He is remembered by one of the city's further education colleges being named after him.

Discrimination in housing and the job market dogged members of the black community and many, such as the Igbo merchant seamen who worked on British ships between Liverpool and West Africa, set up their own self-help community organisations to counter direct prejudice such as the refusal of pubs to serve them. These organisations were also a way to deal with their isolation. By raising levies among themselves the Igbo Union bought a house in Mulgrave Street to use as a meeting place and in the late 1960s bought 54 Princes Road as a club whose proceeds were used for the welfare support of members.

In 1986, not long after the riots in Liverpool in the district known by Liverpudlians as Liverpool 8 but by visiting journalists as Toxteth, a weary deputation from the Merseyside Community Relations Council travelled to Westminster to give evidence to the House of Commons Select Committee on Employment. They felt that they had made all these points before but they made them again in a plea for government to do something about 'the continually devastating problem of massive unemployment facing the black community in Liverpool'. They pointed out that this was a longstanding problem in Liverpool and that the responses to date from both central and local government had been 'shamefully inadequate and irresponsible'. They marshalled statistics to show 'the almost total exclusion of black people from most job oppportunities in Liverpool'. In spite of the fact that this community (and the CRC was using 'black' in its widest sense to cover a range of ethnic groups) amounted to seven or eight per cent of the city's population they formed only one per cent of the local government workforce and one per cent of the workforce in city centre offices and shops. Of 10,000 employees in 19 city centre stores only 75 employees were black and only 10–12 were behind counters. The 'invisibility' of Liverpool's black population was plain enough. The most recent census figures showed a Black British population of 9250 in Liverpool, 3750 Chinese, 3250 West Indian, 3250 Arab, 3000 African and 2500 Asian. Anyone on a shopping spree in the city centre would have seen very few of these.

And in the summer of 2005 a black teenager, Anthony Walker, was murdered by racists in the outer suburb of Huyton in a senseless and ugly piece of bigoted violence. Local community campaigners revealed that in the two months leading up to Anthony Walker's murder 25 reports of attacks on ethnic minorities had been reported. His mother told a newspaper: 'Babies would be calling us niggers and they didn't even understand what they were saying.' The term 'hate crime' – untypical of the usual cautious periphrasis that is used in public policy discussions – is for once a brutally accurate one. Anthony Clarke of the L8 Law Centre told the *Liverpool Daily Post*: 'Racism is alive in every sphere of life in Liverpool'.

At the time of the CRC visit to the House of Lords, Liverpool was being run by a Labour Party faction known as the Militant Tendency whose half-baked 'workerist' ideology led

15

to clashes with representatives of the black community. The Militant leader of Liverpool City Council, Derek Hatton, was half-admired by many who were not his natural ideological soulmates because of his cheeky-chappie Scouse *chutzpah* and his willingness to send a message of defiance both to Margaret Thatcher and to the leadership of his own party. Hatton – 'Deggsie' – was, as Liverpool historian Tony Lane puts it in his *Liverpool: Gateway of Empire* (1987), 'noticed less for his words than his persona'. To nobody's surprise the sharp-suited, mouthy, dapper Hatton, eventually quit and went into the PR business.

There is a long tradition of defiance in Liverpool – speak to any exasperated national trade union official – expressed towards people at the top, even of one's own labour movement organisations. Hatton successfully rode this wave of sympathy for two-fingered bolshieness but there was another, far more powerful symbol of protest against the complacency of what Liverpool's Anglican bishop, David Sheppard, called at the time 'Comfortable Britain'. In the early 1980s a Liverpool playwright who had started his career (having found as a teacher that there was a shortage of relevant reading material for his teenage pupils) writing stories about a streetwise Scouse teenager called Scully wrote a TV play about a gang of tarmac-layers. Alan Bleasdale's *Boys from the Blackstuff* was transmitted in the early 1980s and in spite of his repeated disavowals of political intent, Bleasdale captured and defined a certain moment in recent British culture. The character of Yosser Hughes, with his plaintive lament 'Gizza job', became a national symbol of the desperation of the unemployed, a disproportionate number of whom were to be found in Liverpool. Yosser's almost resigned, desperate follow-up to potential employers, 'I can do that', became a Liverpool catchphrase. When someone was about to take a corner or a penalty kick they bellowed from the Kop: 'I can do that!'

This sense of frustrated capacity, of being denied any chances, was felt by everyone in Liverpool in the 1980s, but was the latest twist of the knife for those who had long been at an extreme disadvantage in the labour market.

In his 1952 autobiography *Chiaroscuro* the painter Augustus John recounted a period he spent in Liverpool (the grotty student campus pub where I frequently supped was called after him!). He had been commissioned to paint a portrait of the Lord Mayor, Chaloner Dowdall, with whom he was staying. Each morning the two of them drove in the official horse-drawn carriage to the Town Hall for the sitting but John was itching for a taste of Bohemian life away from 'the uneventful respectability of Sefton Park'. To the alarm of the Lord Mayor, who feared that his dignity might be compromised, John went off on some nocturnal excursions. 'Liverpool, commonly considered a dull, ugly and commercial city, for me abounded in interest and surprise,' the painter wrote. 'With what wonderment I explored the sombre district of the Mersey side!' Off Scotland Road he 'penetrated, not without trepidation, into the lodging houses of the Tinkers, where a rough, nomadic crew gathered round the communal fire in a spirit of precarious good-fellowship'. He also made for the Chinese quarter of the city, but 'while visiting certain tenebrous dens, I attempted, but failed, to attain the blissful *Kif* in the company of dishevelled and muttering devotees of the Laughing God'.

This view of Chinatown as an exotic place of 'tenebrous dens' was widespread but, although there would certainly have been some opium dealing and using, most of Liverpool's Chinese community was engaged in more workaday pursuits. The original Liverpool Chinatown was confined to an area bounded by Cleveland Square and Pitt Street, but this was already a cosmopolitan area shared with Scandinavian and African seafarers, European Jews, Irish immigrants, Greeks and many others to form what a recent historian of Liverpool's Chinese community, Maria Lin Wong, calls in *Chinese Liverpudlians* (1989) 'this multi-cultural jigsaw'. Chinese sailors first started to arrive in Liverpool in the middle of the nineteenth century. The foundation of the Ocean Steam Ship Company in 1865 and the Blue Funnel Line, the company behind the first direct steamship link between Britain and China which was the largest single employer of Chinese labour, ensured that a regular number of Chinese seamen would settle in Liverpool. During the 1940s Liverpool was the headquarters of the Western Approaches and the home of the Chinese Merchant Seamen's Pool, which meant that up to 20,000 men were registered in the port from Shanghai and the Chinese mainland. Most of the first Chinese settlers in Liverpool before the 1920s were from Guangdong Province and Hong Kong. Guangzhou was the first treaty port in China and the destination of all Liverpool ships.

After the war the Chinese population rose steadily, with most immigrants coming from Hong Kong, as the restaurant trade boomed. It peaked around 1970 as the Chinese began to develop restaurants elsewhere in Europe. Today's Chinatown is centred on the Nelson Street area and the city's Chinese population is around 10,000.

The first activity of the Chinese in Liverpool was the establishment of Chinese boarding houses for seamen. Such Chinese restaurants as existed were at first only for this clientele and it was not until after the war that the prototype of the Chinese restaurant aimed at British tastes opened: Foo Nam Low's in Pitt Street. In the 1950s that now traditional part of Liverpool culture the 'Chinese chippy' appeared, combining traditional fish and chips with Chinese elements such as chop suey roll. There were also Chinese grocers and provision merchants such as Low Chung's in Pitt Street selling such delicacies as tofu cakes and China plums. The other major commercial activity of the Chinese before the dominance of catering was the laundry trade. Chinese laundries were generally run from ordinary terraced houses which combined work and living space and depended crucially on all members of the family of all ages being employed. Apart from occasional adverse press coverage of alleged opium-taking and gambling, together with claims that the laundries were sometimes the cover for brothels, the Chinese experienced only occasional discrimination. As with the black workers noted above during the 1919 race riots, it was fear of economic competition in hard times that fuelled the more serious racist outbreaks. In 1902 Ben Tillet warned in a TUC paper that cheap Chinese labour would threaten the British working man. The TUC, he said, 'could only measure the evil by trying to realise what it would mean to the workmen of this country to have a horde of Chinamen introduced to take their place'.

Smaller communities such as the Jews – by 1852 Liverpool had the largest provincial Jewish community in Britain – and Muslims found their place in the ethnic jigsaw. In the late nineteenth century Liverpool's mosque was the only formally recognised Muslim institution in England and was situated in an ordinary terrace familiar to later generations as the site of the Registry of Births, Deaths and Marriages in Brougham Terrace. About a year before it moved from this location I came there with my mother to register my own father's death.

Because of Liverpool's geographical location – one can see the Welsh hills from certain vantage points in the city – the Welsh were another contributor to the cultural mix. In 1782 at the Pitt Street home of William Llwyd the first Welsh-language prayer meeting took place and the first building exclusively used by the Liverpool Welsh was the Pall Mall Calvinistic Methodist Chapel. In 1884 the Welsh National Eisteddfod was held in Liverpool and there existed a considerable Welsh-language literature from Liverpool, hymning nostalgia and exile. In 1753 the curate at Walton Church, Goronwy Owen, wrote in Welsh to his friend William Morris: 'The people around here, so far as I can see, are but little better than the Hottentots; immoral untamed creatures. When one meets them, they merely stare slyly, saying no more than a cow; yet I hear that they are precocious foxes, wickedly cunning and crafty.' By 1813 one out of every ten people in Liverpool was Welsh and over the next 40 years the Welsh population increased to 40,000, many of whom spoke no English. When Nathaniel Hawthorne worked in Liverpool as American consul he needed to employ an interpreter in order to deal with some Welsh people who came in to his office. In Eleazar Roberts' Liverpool novel *Owen Rees: A Story of Welsh Life and Thought* (1893) one character declares: 'Liverpool and its suburbs can boast of nearly sixty thousand and more than fifty places of worship in which the Welsh language is exclusively used, and, therefore, it may well be described as the capital of Wales.' I am reminded that when I worked in the bar of an Irish country hotel in the summer of 1971 I was frequently told – in response to queries about where I came from – that Liverpool was 'the capital of Ireland'.

There were Welsh sailors, too, and, according to my friend George Nicholson, a former Fifth Engineer on the Blue Funnel ships owned by Alfred Holt & Co., his line was known as the 'Welsh Navy', because of the number of people – particularly from North Wales – who sailed with the company.

Less well publicised than the Liverpool Irish, the Welsh kept themselves a little apart through a network of chapels with associated cultural and financial institutions. They had a strangehold on the Liverpool building industry – many of the streets in parts of the docklands were given Welsh names – and controlled many of that industry's raw material trades such as timber and roofing slate. This combination of cultural self-sufficency and the fact that they were many people's land-lords fuelled a certain amount of resentment, but the Welsh never seem to have been scapegoated like other groups.

Those others included the Italians, Scottish, Asians, Greeks – we shall come to the Irish later – and just about every ethnic community one can think of. The second largest port of Empire after London, Liverpool could not have been anything other than a lively cosmopolitan mix. But outside the wharves and dockside boozers and special streets its minorities remained hardly visible.

3

The Meaning of Scouse

One summer I took a job as a horticultural labourer. Each morning the small gang of three labourers would muster in the yard to find out where the boss – a well-meaning Quaker with an awed reverence for *The Guardian* – was going to take us that day. One sunny morning he announced that we were off to trim the lawns and tidy the flower beds at an old people's home in Knotty Ash. We all erupted into spontaneous laughter. For Knotty Ash is both the home and focal point of the humour of the city's most famous comedian, Ken Dodd – 'the face that launched a thousand quips', as his website informs us.

Born on 8 November 1927 in Knotty Ash, Ken Dodd is an interesting phenomenon in the history of British popular entertainment. Starting out as a traditional end-of-the-pier variety entertainer he seized the opportunity provided by television. His career flourished and still appears to be flourishing as he approaches 80. He has even appeared at the Hay-on-Wye Festival of Literature. He took off as a professional performer in the mid-1950s and did summer seasons at Blackpool in 1955 and 1956, topping the bill there in 1958 at the Central Pier. This led to appearances at the London Palladium and on television. He had his own TV series such as *The Ken Dodd Show* and *Doddy's Music Box* and in the 1960s he developed an additonal career as a singer of romantic ballads. The titles of some of his recordings say it all: 'Love is Like A Violin' (1960), 'Happiness' (1964), 'I Can't Seem to Say Goodbye to You' (1966). This was the sort of stuff that the explosion of Merseybeat and the whole Beatles phenomenon was supposed to have relegated to the dustbin of light entertainment but Doddy wowed them throughout the sixties with these schmaltzy ballads. His 1965 single 'Tears' spent four weeks at the top of the charts, which could not be matched at the time by the Beatles, the Hollies or the Rolling Stones. Moreover, he kept it up for ten years.

But it is the comedy that counts. Dodd represents the softer side of Liverpool comic surrealism. He is no Alexei Sayle. His repertoire of comic characters from Knotty Ash is drawn from the tribe of Diddymen which he invented originally to appeal to children in the audience. 'Diddy' is Scouse for 'little'. Dicky Mint, Mick the Marmaliser, Evan, Hamish McDiddy, and Nigel Ponsonby Smallpiece (check the familiar ethnic and class stereotypes) worked at the Jam Butty Mines in Knotty Ash. In panto the Diddymen are played by children in costume but for his stage act Dodd used just a puppet of Dicky Mint, with whom he did a ventriloquist routine. Another of his properties is the tickling stick, which looks a bit like a feather duster. The jokes are Liverpool jokes. At the Liverpool Empire he looks up at the people in the gods and announces: 'It's a privilege to be asked to play here tonight on what is a very special anniversary. It's a hundred years to the night since that balcony collapsed.' The asides to the audience, the women always addressed as 'Missus', the daft routines, the puns, the old jokes (he famously keeps copious notebooks of jokes classified according to what will work where), the cracks about the Inland Revenue, with whom he had a famous confrontation and court case ('Self-assessment – they stole the idea from me'), add up to a style of comedy that is almost certainly on its way out and that is utterly removed from the patter you hear in the fashionable London comedy clubs listed in *Time Out*. There's a common quip you hear in Liverpool after some possibly less than Wildean witticism: 'Well, it made *me* laugh.' This is impossible to translate but means something like: 'This may not be regarded as funny by anyone applying strict canons of criticism, especially people who live south of Watford, but I have decided it's funny and that's all that matters as far as I am concerned. Don't think you or anyone else can lecture me about what is or is not funny. You'd be wasting your breath. It's my freedom to laugh at whatever I like.'

Ken Dodd has occasionally made *me* laugh.

As well as the official jokers (I pass over another *Sunday Night at the London Palladium* compère, Norman Vaughan, who was taught by my Auntie Winnie at English Martyrs RC Primary, and whose catchphrase was 'Very dodgy') there is a whole field of linguistic invention that one hears on the street and which has passed into the lexicon of Scouse. The word 'Scouse', by the way, probably derives from the Scandinavian word *labskaus* or lobscouse, which turns up in some eighteenth-century texts such as Tobias Smollett's *Peregrine Pickle*, where it mutates into 'Lob's course'. The chief point to grasp about this dish called Scouse is that you would not want to eat it if you had access to anything better. Here is a recipe, quoted by Gladys Mary Coles in her anthology *Both Sides of the River*, and used by the Birkenhead workhouse in 1864: '1oz beef, 15oz potatoes, 1 gall water. Cut up and boil. Serve 2 lbs to men and 1 and a half pounds to women.' If you couldn't afford meat you ate 'blind scouse'. Fortunately this dull stew isn't served anywhere in Liverpool today as far as I can establish. Since you are what you eat, a Liverpudlian is a 'Scouser', but none I think would touch this stew if they could possibly avoid it.

In 1966 the musician and wit Fritz Spiegl produced a guide to Scouse called *Lern Yerself Scouse: How to Talk Proper in Liverpool*, a book which is still on sale in the city and which can be supplemented by Diana Briscoe's more recent *Wicked Scouse English* (2003). Spiegl was the Royal Liverpool Philharmonic Orchestra flautist who, with Bridget Fry, arranged an old Liverpool sea shanty, 'Johnny Todd' (which I often sing in the shower) to be the signature tune for a new TV police series of the 1960s called *Z Cars*:

Johnny Todd he took a notion
For to cross the ocean wide
And he left his love behind him
Weeping on the Liverpool side.

He thought that the playful inventiveness of Scouse was an echo of Viennese *Schlamperei* ('easy going untidiness combined with a lazy amiability') and that 'the engaging slovenliness of Scouse speech results in an entirely characteristic use of the shortest possible diminutives'. But there was also 'Scouse circumlocution', whereby, instead of compression, there is a wonderful expansion that makes Anfield Cemetery 'De Anfield Bone Orcherd' or a black Liverpudlian 'a smoked Irishman'. Spiegl insisted that the latter was not offensive or racist but rather showed a spirit of jokey and benevolent acceptance. The diminutives he noted are often applied to people's names. We have already encountered 'Deggsie' Hatton and my father was amused when at school I was given the same nickname that he had received at St

25

James's, Bootle, just after the First World War: 'Muggsie'. I have a very old friend from my earliest schooldays, a respectable public relations practitioner on Merseyside, who to this day greets me as 'Niggsie' when we meet. 'It's cold enough fer two pur a bootlaces' is Spiegl's phonetic attempt to capture the suggestion that the weather is very cold. Many single words seem to be unique to Liverpool but there is always the possibility that they are shared elsewhere. The alley or entry that runs between two rows of terraced houses is a 'jigger' and policemen are 'scuffers'. Trousers are 'kecks' and best clothes for a formal occasion 'bezzies'. Bare feet are 'bare webs' and the raspberry sauce sluiced over ice-cream cornets served up from mobile vans was in my schooldays 'bug-juice'. A packed lunch is 'a carry-out' and a pastry with currant filling is 'fly pie'. Practising *coitus interruptus* is 'getting off at Edge Hill' (the last stop before Lime Street terminus). Liverpool is the only place in the English-speaking world where you can refer to your girlfriend affectionately as 'me tart' without creating entirely the wrong impression or being clouted with her handbag. A talkative woman is said to have 'a mouth like a parish oven' and I remember someone at school telling a classmate 'You've got an 'ead as big as Birkenhead and a mouth as big as the Mersey Tunnel'. Some phrases may contain some lost history, such as 'when Donnelly docked' meaning 'a long time ago'. Replying to a severe question from my father about whether I had carried out some instruction to the letter I said I thought I had done it correctly, to which he responded: 'You know what thought did. Went behind a muck-cart and thought it was a wedding.'

There is a streak of self-consciousness about some of the language-games, as when older people like my uncles and aunts would joke about past hard times, recalling a phrase used when a neighbour's husband was home from his voyage with enough money to lash out on extra groceries: 'Your auld man's home? I seen the eggshells in the ashbin.' A tall man, according to Spiegl, 'could wind der Liver clock', and the rough dockland area of the Dingle was 'whur dey play Tick wid Atchets'. New phrases are being added all the time. Frederick Gibberd's new Catholic cathedral, built only in my lifetime, was immediately christened 'Paddy's Wigwam' or 'the Mersey Funnel', both playing on its distinctive shape. Perhaps one of the most characteristic Scouse calls is: 'Cum 'ed!', which means something like 'I say, it's time we were getting a move on, old chap'. And so it goes on.

I am conscious that, when venturing into the definition of 'Scouse' and its attendant humour, I am entering a minefield. One easily exposes oneself to the charge of stereotyping. And much of the humour and larkiness that seemed to dominate my childhood may now be less in evidence. In some ways Liverpool is a less funny place than it was when I was a child, but I still find the old spirit alive as soon as I am back in the city. Some of this is to do with such solemn accolades as being a European Capital of Culture. Walking up Bold Street, one of my stern lecturers on stereotyping recently informed me, one could now imagine oneself in Paris. But why on earth would a unique place like Liverpool want to transform its streets into a second-rate imitation of the Boulevard Saint-Germain? The leader of Liverpool City Council, Councillor Warren Bradley, recently told a local government publication about the 'phenomenal renaissance' of a city which until recently had been in 'terminal decline'. He claimed that what was happening was 'one of the biggest urban transformations ever seen in this country'. It turned out he was talking about shopping. The true meaning of that term 'culture' was at last emerging. Move over, Matthew Arnold. The biggest retail development currently being built in Europe, covering

42 acres – the equivalent of 22 football pitches – was being constructed around Paradise Street (down which we shall be strolling later). This is the centrepiece, the shining *omphalos*, of the Capital of Culture. The heroic Bradley, shamed at his city's humiliating fall to seventeenth place in Britain's shopping league table, was fighting back like Roland at the pass of Roncevaux. By 2008, he predicted, 'Thousands of visitors from throughout the world will be descending on the city and they will have one of Europe's most exciting developments to greet them'.

Meanwhile, I can't help feeling that a few expensive lofts and some tubular steel café tables and chairs aren't enough to remake a city. Sometimes, at my most wicked, I have a dream of a long slow cavalcade of black cars moving through Liverpool's city centre containing the elite guard of the New Humourlessness. They are all there behind the tinted windows: the cultural entrepreneurs, the talkers-up, the PR executives, poets, estate agents, arts funding junkies, hired celebrities, marketing babblers. In my dream I find myself bawling out uncouthly: 'Yer norron!'

Much ink has been spilt on the question of where Liverpool got its name. To start back to front, the pool is obvious from the old maps, which show a distinct inlet which subsequent building and dock construction have obliterated entirely. Boats were built in this upper creek or pool until the authorities ruled that no more boats should be built at Frog Lane – the site of the present Haymarket and Whitechapel. As late as 1758 a 32-gun frigate called the *Venus* was built and launched there. In 1768, when the tide still flowed to the bottom of Water Street, Moor Street, and James Street, before the George's Dock was constructed, a ship riding at anchor was blown over the beach, running her bowsprit through the middle window of the corner house in James Street.

In 1586 William Camden explained in his *Brittania* that the Mersey 'opens into a very wide mouth very commodious for trade, and then runs into the sea, near Litherpoole, in Saxon Liferpole, commonly called Lirpoole, called so (as 'tis thought) from the water spread like a fen there. It is the most convenient and frequented place for setting sail into Ireland'. An earlier historian, John Leland, in 1533, also mentioned the Irish merchants who 'cum much hither as to a good haven' and termed it 'Lyrpole, alias Lyverpoole'. Five different spellings and we have only reached 1586. It seems pretty obvious that 'Lither' or its variants signifies low-lying – as in the case of Litherland, the district in the north of the city where Siegfried Sassoon was in barracks in the First World War. From the higher vantage points in the city, looking down towards the docks, Paradise Street and Whitechapel, under which the old Pool (and the river itself) once lay, are clearly in a low-lying position. But the old antiquarians played with some other possibilities. Might it derive from a seaweed known in some parts of Britain as liver, or from a species of hepatica called liverwort? Or an ancient family in the area, the Levers? Or was the liver a bird? The anonymous author of *A General and Descriptive History of the Ancient and Present State of the Town of Liverpool* (1795) was interested in this liver bird which forms part of the ancient seal and which, famously, crowns the towers of the Liver Buildings on the waterfront today: 'the leading question appears to be, whether this bird is to be placed in the utopian ornithology, with the phoenix, or in reality existed?' This author wonders if it could have been a widgeon, or teal, easterling 'or other species of wild duck'. Warming to his speculations, he mused that the large inlet or pool could have been a decoy for the duck, as elsewhere along the coast, or maybe its migratory residence. Or again, 'in the infant state of the town', the place might have been called *'Liver's Pool,*

29

or pond, to which place the inhabitants might have applied to pursue and catch [duck] for the use of their families'. One of the more inventive hypotheses was that it came from the Welsh 'Lle'r pwll'. This is floated by James Stonehouse in his *The Stranger in Liverpool* (1807), but he then goes on to admit that most of the guesses about the etymology, particularly the ornithological ones, are 'totally destitute of proof'. Not even the usual solution to such disputes – ask the locals – works. In 1173 Henry II referred to Liverpool, in a document granting it all liberties as 'a port of the sea', as 'the place which the men of Lyrpul call Litherpul'. So, although as late as 1770 in his *Essay Towards the History of Leverpool* William Enfield fought a rearguard action, the modern spelling of Liverpool was firmly established during the eighteenth century and the meaning of 'low-lying [or lower] pool' seems – with all due deference to the happy inventiveness of Jung – to be the most obvious one.

Which leaves us only with the Liver Birds.

Enfield observes that 'this bird does not appear to have had any existence except in fabulous tradition and in the herald's office'. When the grant of a new coat of arms was made in 1797 the heraldic description was as follows: 'Argent a Cormorant in the beak a branch of seaweed called Laver all proper, and for the Crest, on a wreath of the colours a Cormorant, the wings elevated, in the beak a branch of Laver proper'. Older seals showed a bird with a twig in its beak, which raises the speculation that it might have been modelled on the eagle of St John the Divine carrying a broom sprig. But today's liver bird, in coppery green form on the top of the Liver Buildings on the waterfront, looks very like a cormorant to me and a piece of laver (a type of seaweed) in its beak is equally plausible. The birds are an arresting symbol. Even the wires that have been placed there to secure them seem like a kind of restraint in case they were minded suddenly to beat their wings and fly out across the river. As one comes towards the Liver Buildings just at dusk, from the south along Wapping, they are etched magnificently against the sky, two dark silhouettes, watching over the city.

4

Through Other Eyes

The first visitor to Liverpool to set down a record of his passing through was John Leland in the sixteenth century. His planned *History and Antiquities of this Nation* never got written but from his mass of notes on that project the posthumously edited *Itinerary* was published in 1710. Around 1533 he came to Liverpool to find 'a pavid Towne, [that] hath but a chapel. The King hath a Castelet there, and the Erle of Darbe a Stone Howse there. Irisch Marchauntes cum much hither as to a good Haven.' And that was it. Liverpool was not even a parish, its fourteenth-century church of St Nicholas only a chapel-of-ease of the parish of Walton, three miles to the north, run by the Benedictine monks of Shrewsbury Abbey. There was also an earlier chapel of Our Lady of the Quays, demolished, like so many of Liverpool's antiquities, in the nineteenth century (even the city's current proudest 'heritage' boast, the magnificent Albert Dock, nearly fell to the demolition ball in the 1970s). The fourteenth-century castle referred to by Leland is also long gone. In 1533 there was no hint of the massive seven miles of docks and the seaport's later teeming life which started to erupt in the seventeenth century as it exploited its advantages, facing west, and drawing from its hinterland the exports of the nascent industrial revolution in the north and midlands. The first recorded cargo from America – thirty tons of tobacco – arrived in 1648 and before the end of the seventeenth century sugar from the West Indies was already being refined in the Dale Street area.

In 1586 William Camden concluded that Liverpool was 'a town more famous for its beauty and populousness than its antiquity', sounding a constant theme of later historians: the absence of visible remains of its mediaeval past. It is a city with a foreshortened history. In the city's records is an order issued to the burgesses in 1571 'to attend the mayor on the midsummer eve's walk, St Peter's Day, and the two fair days, in their best apparel [their 'bezzies'] and with their best weapons, as of old'.

In 1698 the diarist Celia Fiennes arrived to record a vitality that echoes what the sculptor Jacob Epstein, two and a half centuries later, in his famous post-war naked scuplture on the Lewis's department store would call *The Spirit of Liverpool Resurgent*. The port was now bustling, with the first Liverpool slave ship taking to the sea the year after her visit. Celia Fiennes found

> mostly new built houses of brick and stone after the London fashion; the first original was a few fishermens houses and now is grown to a large fine town... a great many Dessenters in the town; its a very rich trading town the houses of brick and stone built high and even, that a streete quite through lookes very handsome, the streets well pitched; there are abundance of persons you see very well dress'd and of good fashion; the streets are faire and long, its London in miniature as much as ever I saw any thing; there is a very pretty Exchange stands on 8 pillars besides the corners which are treble pillars all of stone and its railed in over which is a

> very handsome Town Hall; over all is a tower and cupillow
> thats so high that from thence one has the whole view of
> the town and the country round; in a clear day you may see
> the Isle of Man...

The Liverpool Exchange and its surrounding 'Flags', receiving their first pen-portrait here, would be a central feature of future accounts, though the buildings would be regularly rebuilt – right through to George Garrett's memorable description of their invasion by the angry unemployed in 1921. In other respects Fiennes' account is not typical, however, for in later centuries descriptions of Liverpool would increasingly focus not on the city's elegance and 'good fashion' but on the growing urban squalor.

By the time that Daniel Defoe arrived in Liverpool in 1721, on a ferry from the Wirral, as part of his *Tour Through the Whole Island of Great Britain*, the port was booming:

> *Liverpoole* is one of the wonders of *Britain*, because of its
> prodigious Increase of Trade and Buildings, within the
> Compass of a very Few Years; rivalling *Bristol* in the Trade
> to *Virginia*, and the *English* Colonies in *America*. They trade
> also round the whole Island; send ships to *Norway* and
> *Flanders*; so that they are almost become, like the *Londoners*,
> universal Merchants.

Defoe estimated that Liverpool's commerce had increased tenfold during the seventeenth century and he was impressed by the port's ability to combine a commercial shrewdness and economy with the display of 'surprising Spirit in Works of large Expence, for the improvement of the Town and Port'. He noted how, in spite of a good harbour, the ships had originally been required to anchor in the river. 'Here was no Mole or Haven to bring in their Ships, and lay them up (as the Seamen call it) for the Winter, nor any Quay for the delivering of their Goods, as at *Bristol, Bidiford, Newcastle, Hull*, and other Sea-ports.' So the enterprising Liverpudlians constructed 'a large Basin, or Wet-dock, at the East End of the Town, where at very great Charge, the Place considered, they have brought the Tide from the *Mersey*, to flow up by an Opening, that looks to the South, and the Ships go in North; so that the Town shelters it from the Westerly and Northerly Winds, the Hills from the Easterly, and the Ships lie as in a Mill-pond, with the utmost Safety and Convenience.' Defoe noted that the dock (which was built in 1715 and was the first commercial enclosed wet dock in the world) was capable of holding a hundred ships and that the entrance to the dock had been widened, a pier built, and lighting installed to deter smugglers. He, too, praised the Exchange and the 'Piazzas for the Merchants to walk in' around it. 'In a Word, there is no Town in *England*, except *Manchester*, that can equal *Liverpoole* for the Fineness of the Streets, and Beauty of the Buildings.'

Today the only survival of that eighteenth-century elegance is the Bluecoat Chambers, the former Bluecoat School, whose enclosed rear garden is a welcome space of tranquillity for those city centre *flâneurs* who know about it. One writer, 'Dicky Sam', described a rather more sylvan scene around 1760 than anything now to be found in Liverpool (though on a recent visit I was surprised on a piece of waste ground near Paradise Street by a pair of goldfinches feeding on the fluffy top of a thistle):

> The end of Duke Street terminated in fields and green trees, whilst here and there stood many picturesque wind-mills overlooking the busy scenes in the town below. Lime Street and the London Road were in the country, and cattle might have been seen grazing amid the buttercups and daisies. The thickly populated north end of the town was fields; fields everywhere.

One eighteenth-century building that no longer exists, sadly, is the Institution for Restoring Drowned Persons which opened in 1775. The anonymous author of *The Picture of Liverpool or Stranger's Guide* (1805) explains how it had managed to rescue over 400 people since its inception:

> This extraordinary success has happened from the ready assistance which is always at hand about the docks and the river. A guinea is given to those who take up a body, if it be afterwards restored to life; if not restored half-a-guinea. It is at the Corporation expense. Long poles with hooks at the ends, are dispersed in different places about the docks, for the purpose of dragging for those persons who fall in.

Another vanished remnant of the eighteenth century is the phenomenon of Liverpool pottery. This distinctive porcelain flourished as one of the town's main industries until competition from Staffordshire ware more or less finished it off. According to its historian, Knowles Boney, 'no chinaware of comparable importance...is less well known'. In 1701 a Josiah Poole first received permission from the Corporation to make tiles and pantiles and brick from local clay but the manufacture of the distinctive Liverpool delftware soon became established. Local potter John Sadler is said to have invented the transfer technique for decorating pottery when he gave his children some spoiled impressions from his engraved plates. He found that they were sticking these onto pieces of broken pottery, which gave him the idea of using paper transfers from engraved plates. His success puzzled his rivals, who could not understand how a rigid copper plate could be made to give an impression on a curved surface. Around the middle of the century Sadler tried to patent the technique but his claim to have invented it was disputed, though Wedgwood was among those who sent tiles to be printed by Sadler.

In the early eighteenth century pottery manufacture was one of the most important industries in Liverpool and exports to America and elsewhere formed the basis of the trade. In the latter half of the century jugs began to be very popular and were generally decorated with nautical patterns. During the American War of Independence cream-coloured jugs – 'yellow ware' or 'Liverpool ware' – were sent in great numbers to America with mottoes, inscriptions, likenesses and views relating to America and leading American celebrities. American shipowners often ordered from Liverpool potters pieces representing pictures of their own vessels. One of the best known potteries making them was the Herculaneum Pottery, whose eventual demise in 1840 marked the end of the trade in Liverpool. In Alice Morse's *China Collecting in America* there is a story of an old New England woman who brought out to show the author 'a pair of small Liverpool pitchers printed with a spirited marine view of a full-rigged ship', the names John Daggett and Eliza Maxom, and this doggerel rhyme:

No more I'll roam,
I'll stay at home,
To sail no more
From shore to shore,
But with my wife
Lead a happy and peaceful life.

The old woman said that the sailor, John Daggett, 'ordered 'em painted for him and me in Liverpool on the last trip he ever went on. He was the han'somest man ye ever see! He died on the voyage home.'

More indifferent late-eighteenth-century poetry was spouted in June 1772 at the grand opening of Liverpool's new Theatre Royal in Williamson Square by the actor George Colman:

When Caesar first these regions did explore,
And northward his triumphant eagle bore
[did Fatman and Algernon know something after all?]
Rude were Britannia's sons, a hardy race
Their faith idolatry, their life the chace...
Long too has Mersey roll'd her golden tide,
And seen proud vessels in her harbour's ride;
Oft on her banks the Muses's sons would roam,
And wish'd to settle there a certain home.

There is, unfortunately, rather more of this. Much more fun sound the popular street entertainments and festivals of the eighteenth century. On 25th July and 11th November each year Liverpool Fair was held near the Exchange. Several symbolic properties were brought out on these occasions. A carved wooden hand was fastened to the façade of the Exchange for the duration of the Fair. On fair days the mayor, bailiffs, and burgesses in their ceremonial gowns went in procession, accompanied by a band, from the Exchange to the middle of Dale Street, where they passed round a large, whitewashed stone (I have not been able to ascertain the significance of either of these symbols) before moving on to another stone in the centre of Castle Street. They then proceeded back to the Exchange where the Corporation laid on a public dinner for 'the principal inhabitants'.

They would have had no excuse for not dining well. In 1773, William Enfield published 'A TABLE OF FISH taken and sold at Liverpool' which listed 44 varieties including porpoise, sea frog, lamprey, sparling, shad, crubbin, sea spider, sea egg and garr fish, as well as more familiar varieties. The river, in spite of the growing volume of trade, must have been sufficiently clean to sustain all these species. Enfield also set out a table of imports for the year 1770 which shows, from Barbados for example, 'Archelia, Bees' Wax, Cotton, Camwood, Elephants'

Teeth, Ginger, Gum, Guinea Cloths, Hogshead Staves, Madeira Wine, Palm Oil, Rum, Sugar'. Other West Indian imports – some of which I confess to being baffled by – were coffee, cocoa nuts, cotton, balsam, cow hides, cow horns, fustic, indigo, lignum vitae, mahogany, pimento, tortoise shell, cedar, shruff, succades, and ox horns. In the other direction went ale, bricks, bacon, beer, candles, cheese, worsted caps, coals, frying pans, gloves, gun powder, herrings, iron pots, linen, leather, oats, potatoes, pipes, salt, stockings, sail cloth, soap, twine, and woollens. Liverpool at this time sustained no fewer than 27 windmills 'in or very near the town', and 15 roperies. Business was booming.

While the burgesses dined off lamprey and sea spider, the lower orders had their own festive entertainment, the Folly Fair, in lanes near London Road and Folly Lane (present-day Islington). But most intriguing of all is the custom of 'Lifting'. This took place on Easter Monday when groups of men would approach women in the street and seize hold of them in order to toss them up into the air and catch them, sometimes several times. On Easter Tuesday the women would get their revenge by attacking the men with equal vigour. The custom may have had some symbolic meaning alluding to the resurrection or ascension of Christ. The only way to escape this practice, according to Richard Brooke, author of *Liverpool as it Was During the Last Quarter of the Eighteenth Century* (1853), was when the marked victim 'purchased impunity by a pecuniary gratuity'. Another piece of fun took place on Shrove Tuesday when a cock was released at Waterworth's Field near Lime Street in front of a number of boys, whose hands were tied behind their back. They would chase the cock and try to catch it by surrounding it or throwing themselves on it and securing it with their teeth. Whoever succeeded in doing so became the winner.

On 10th October a bear was baited at the white cross, at the top of Chapel Street, and then led in triumph to the Exchange where the process was repeated. The ugly sport is described by Thomas Troughton in his *History of Liverpool from the Earliest Authenticated Period Down to the Present Time* (1810):

> a repetition of the same brutal cruelties were exhibited in Derby-street, and the diversion was concluded by the animal undergoing reiterated assaults at the Stocks-market, opposite the top of Pool-lane. The bear was assailed separately by large mastiffs, and if any dog compelled him to yell, or was able to sustain the contest with superior address, he was rewarded with a brass collar... every house in the vicinity of the spot where the bear was baited, was adorned by the appearance of the most elegant ladies and gentlemen in town, and several of the inhabitants have been known to have obtained from ten to fifteen pounds for the use of their windows during the week of this grand exhibition.

More raucous still appear to have been the annual West Derby wakes during which large numbers of people descended on what was then the village of West Derby accompanied by a collection of terriers, mastiffs and bulldogs. A post was driven into the ground and a strong, fierce bull tied to it with a chain. The bull was then baited by each of the dogs in turn. At the end of this show, Thomas Troughton reports, 'the bull was brought back to Liverpool in triumph, on the evening of the last day of the wakes, his head decorated with ribbons of different colours, with a band of music, a pantaloon, scaramouch, harlequin and other vagabond players attending in his train'. On one notorious occasion in 1783 a party of sailors, armed with swords and bludgeons, led the bull back to town and brought it into one of the boxes at the Theatre Royal to roars from the theatre crowd.

It was at the Theatre Royal, on 8th August 1798, that a London actor, John Palmer, acting in a play called *The Stranger*, delivered the line 'O! God, God! There is another and a better world', and expired. It was some time before the audience realised that his death had been real.

On 20 July 1785 Liverpool witnessed its first balloon flight. Vincent Lunardi set off from the now demolished fort and repeated the experiment on 9th August. According to the historian Henry Smithers, writing in 1825:

> Since that period, numerous aerial flights have been made, by other aeronauts, without having in the least diminished public curiosity; for, whenever any ascent is about to take place, the whole town appears in agitation; the shops are, for the most part, closed; the counting-houses deserted; and the major part of the population spread over the adjoining country, in such directions as the balloon is likely to take. Horsemen, ready mounted, follow its course with a speed resembling the coursers at a steeple hunt.

It was the view of later writers such as Troughton, however, that the lower orders were showing their true colours: 'A disgusting vulgarity of manners prevailed among the lower class of society in Liverpool at this period', he complained. This would become an increasingly vocal lament of observers and commentators on the city. 'The streets of Liverpool,' declared Richard Brooke, looking back from 1853 and the unassailable position of mid-Victorian middle-class respectability, 'frequently exhibited sad scenes of profligacy; abandoned women paraded them in considerable numbers, indulging in disgusting language, noises, and riotous conduct, without any effectual interference from the police.' Another historian, the anonymous author of *A General and Descriptive History of the Ancient and Present State of the Town of Liverpool* (1795), reported:

It is no unusual thing to see a great number of girls, and may of the inferior inhabitants of the town, assembled in the evenings at various diversions, in the narrow streets and outlets of the town, to the great annoyance of such of the inhabitants as are disposed to a peaceable and quiet residence, even the squares are not exempt from this nuisance, where it is common to see boys and girls playing at ball, and other diversions, every Sunday afternoon.

Some of the above behaviour can still be witnessed in Liverpool city centre on a Friday night, particularly when the hen parties are in full cry.

Brooke regretted that '[the] amusements and habits of the lower classes in Liverpool were then rude and coarse. Drunkenness was a common vice, and was indulged in without concealment.'

The natives call it 'going on the bevvy'.

5

The Africa Trade

It matters how we arrive at a city.

First impressions can be indelible and even the most exciting and enchanting cities can fail us if we get off on the wrong foot. I first arrived at Marseilles at dawn, on a magnificent white ferry from Ajaccio in Corsica called – what else? – the *Napoleon Buonaparte*. The gentle morning sunlight bathed the honey-coloured stone of the harbour outworks in a lovely glow. Everyone crowded into the bows of our faintly preposterous floating tower-block of a ship to catch the moment of arrival. Nothing else in the city subsequently lived up to this arrival but had I reached it by car or bus the impact would have been even more diminishing. Arriving at Zagreb's magnificent railway station, faced by a long prospect of green where a band was playing, no subsequent experience of the city's less elegant parts could persuade me that it was anything other than a stylish and civilised capital. Disembarking from a Malaysian train at Singapore and passing through a narrow tunnel, one side of which consisted of wire mesh against which dogs trained to sniff out illegal drugs hurled themselves in pent-up aggression, ensured that I would never be enchanted by that hygienically authoritarian enclave of South East Asia. My first sight of Sofia was the late night railway station and the surrounding streets in which half the lights were out and where the proprietor of the first hotel I came to delivered a stern warning about not carrying too much money when I went out. Next day, I went about with some apprehension, justified by a quick razor slash of my backpack, which fortunately contained no valuables. The pleasant squares, the solemn chess-players in the municipal parks, the cheerful flower-women in the streets, could not counter that first, unpleasant stumble into the city. And as for arriving from the bright colour of Bali at Perth, Australia on a deserted Anzac day...

As far as Liverpool is concerned, I was never granted that option of a first impression. Having been born in the city I wasn't offered the chance to develop a perspective. Sometimes I play with the conceit that I simply forced my way up through a gap in the paving stones and started walking. I am an obsessive *flâneur*. I have come to judge cities by their capacity to accommodate the pedestrian, the idle stroller, the person without a vehicle on wheels who wants time to look around, to gaze up at a window, a pediment, an architectural oddity, the expressive faces of the passing crowd. Walking is the truly civilised activity of the urban animal. Preparing to write this book I spent time in Liverpool, trying to make myself an outsider, a rubbernecker, my copy of Joseph Sharples' essential *Liverpool* Pevsner guide in my hand (or hidden furtively in a carrier bag), walking in circles, through old haunts, past buildings that triggered memories (the magnificent *art nouveau* Philharmonic Hotel, for example, where the Liverpool Poets used to prop up the bar), tut-tutting at the dereliction of parts of the city centre such as London Road or Hanover Street, along most of one side of which empty, crumbling buildings, sprouting purple cones of buddleia, cry out for something to be done to them. As we have seen, Councillor Warren Bradley has heard the cry. His 22 football pitches' worth of shopping mall will do the trick. With the original plan to build a vast architectural symbol (all fur coat and no knickers) next to the 'Three Graces' (the Liver Building, the Cunard Building, and the former Mersey Docks and Harbour Board Building) on the waterfront now seemingly in tatters maybe a revamped Hanover Street will at last connect the city centre to the Albert Dock and the waterfront that it seems to have turned its back on.

Walking around the city centre, catching those wonderful chance views of the cathedrals, the Liver Building and so forth which suddenly appear as one turns a corner or sprints across a road, and feeling a sense of space and amplitude which overcrowded, dense, hurrying London cannot match, one can see how, with the right kind of vision, so much could be done to re-animate the urban landscape.

Visitors to Liverpool have arrived by steamer from America (Melville, Hawthorne) or by local ferry (Defoe, the Rev. Francis Kilvert) or by train from Euston (Matthew Arnold, Virginia Woolf) – nobody has managed to make poetry of arrival out of the motorway box. All have been ready to record their immediate impressions. Nobody, it seems, has been indifferent to the city.

On 20th August 1797, the diarist the Reverend William Bagshaw Stevens, headmaster of Repton, arrived at Liverpool by sea. He was at first detained by a contrary wind but eventually he docked and marvelled at the 1200 ships the docks contained. His journal entry, however, was brief and pungent: 'Throughout this large-built Town, every Brick is cemented to its fellow Brick by the blood and sweat of Negroes.' Stevens had grasped the essential point about the source of Liverpool's wealth and commanding position. He looked over a ship bound for Guinea which was capable of holding 450 slaves and which had made for its owners, in the last year, at 1797 prices, a cool £7000. Although Stevens was not alone in being repelled by this vile trade, the Liverpool merchants, the Corporation, and all the city's Members of Parliament, with the exception of the abolitionist William Roscoe, did everything in their power throughout the century to fight abolition. And even as late as 1957, a history of Liverpool commissioned by the City Corporation managed to dismiss the topic in a couple of paragraphs, arguing that it 'was to bring benefits to all'.

Although the slave trade began in the late sixteenth century it was not until 1698 when Parliament scrapped the monopoly enjoyed by the Royal African Company that the trade opened up. Liverpool saw its chance and within two years, in September 1700, the first slave ship, the *Liverpool Merchant*, set sail, carrying goods to West Africa where 200 slaves were bought and taken to Barbados (via the notorious 'middle passage'), where they were sold for £4239. The ships returned with goods from the West Indies, completing a triangular trade which, as one commentator put it, yielded three profits in one voyage, and which also kept the slaves, and the inhumanity of their treatment, well out of the consciousness of Liverpool society, though the ship's chandler's shops of the city were to display in their windows, as the century progressed, a range of shackles, thumbscrews, branding irons, and devices for opening the mouths of slaves when they refused to eat. In October, another boat, the *Blessing*, sailed from Liverpool and the trade was fully launched. At the start of the eighteenth century London dominated the British slave trade but by the 1720s Bristol had taken the lead. By the 1740s, however, Liverpool had overtaken both ports. By the 1780s nearly twice as many slaving ships left Liverpool each year as from London and Bristol combined. All but three of the 19 most important British firms engaged in slave trading were based in Liverpool. The port controlled 60 per cent of the British slave trade and over 40 per cent of the entire European slave trade. By the time the slave trade was abolished in 1807 over 90 per cent of all slave ships cleared from Liverpool.

A range of geographical and industrial factors contributed to Liverpool's success in what was euphemistically called 'the Africa trade'. As the historians of Liverpool's slave trade, Gail Cameron and Stan Cooke, put it: 'The opening years of the eighteenth century saw a significant development of manufacturing in Liverpool's hinterland of Lancashire, Cheshire, and Staffordshire. The looms, foundries, and workshops which were established in these years produced the cloth, iron bars, pans, cutlery, weapons and gunpowder with which slaves in Africa were purchased.' Liverpool was increasingly linked to these industrial centres by the new network of waterways. The Bridgewater Canal, for example, gave it a distinct advantage over Bristol. Lancashire products such as cotton, wool, copper, and pewter were bartered on the Guinea coast for slaves, gold dust and elephants' teeth and, after the slaves were disposed of in Jamaica, rum and sugar were brought back in the ships. The merchants were determined to preserve this lucrative business. 'The merchants and political dignitaries of Liverpool,' observe Cameron and Cooke, 'campaigned untiringly for free trade in unfree labour.' When the trade was finally abolished the accumulated capital laid the basis for the city's nineteenth-century economic growth.

The actual conditions for slaves were terrifying. Diagrams exist of slave ships showing the human cargo stowed like anchovies in a tin and many did not survive the voyage. 'Be very careful in the beginning of your purchase,' the captain of the Sally was told in 1768, 'that the slaves be choice and such as will stand, for you know that they will be considerably longer on board and are to stand the whole purchase.' In the middle passage the death rate was around one in twelve. The slaves were crushed together below decks, sometimes with shelves installed halfway up the walls to accommodate yet more slaves, and generally without sufficient space to lie on their backs. The stench and foul air was made worse in rough seas when portholes were closed and they were lucky to be taken up on deck once a day.

In his *Liverpool and Slavery: An Historical Account of the Liverpool–African Slave Trade* (1884) the anonymous author who calls himself the obsolete name that once signified a native Scouser, 'Dicky Sam', furnished a horrifying description of conditions below deck on the middle passage:

> So small was the space allowed to each, they had not so much room as a man in a coffin. They were placed lying on their back, and sometimes they were packed spoonways, one on the other; so close were they, you could not walk without treading on them, but then they were only slaves. One kind-hearted sailor, when passing over them, would remove his shoes so as not to hurt them. So close and foul was the stench arising from the negroes, they have been known to be put down the hold strong and healthy at night; and have been dead in the morning. A trader stated that after remaining ten minutes in the hold, his shirt was as wet as if it had been in a bucket of water.

Dicky Sam also describes a typical daily routine on a slaver. At eight in the morning, the seas permitting, the slaves would be brought up on deck chained together by ring bolts fastened to the deck to prevent them jumping overboard. They were fed on raw yams and 'horse beans' served out twice daily with half a pint of water after each meal. Sick or dying slaves were thrown overboard for the sharks which often followed the slave vessels. After being fed the slaves were called on to jump – as often as not to the music of a cat o' nine tails – in order to keep healthy. A report of this reached Liverpool, where it was interpreted as evidence that the slaves were happy and dancing for joy.

Liverpool slave traders committed some of the worst atrocities against slaves. Captain Marshall of the *Black Joke* flogged a baby to death for refusing food and then forced the child's mother to throw the corpse overboard. Captain Collingwood on the slaver *Zong*, owned by the prominent Liverpool banker William Gregson, had 133 slaves thrown overboard in order to claim compensation for 'loss of merchandise'. Even if the slaves survived the passage one in three died within three years of arrival in the Americas from disease. Not every slave trader, however, was as monstrous as Marshall and Collingwood. The one-eyed Manxman, Captain Hugh Crow, treated his slaves so well (by comparison) that he was astonished to receive a visit on his ship at Kingston, Jamaica, from a deputation of former slaves who chanted: 'God bless Massa!'

Like William Gregson, Liverpool's slave traders belonged to the most powerful and affluent sections of Liverpool society. 'All the great old Liverpool families were more or less steeped in the slave trade,' wrote Dicky Sam. 'Liverpool may be looked upon as the slave town of the old world.' Many Liverpool street names commemorate men who made their fortunes from the slave trade or were vigorous advocates of it: Bamber Street (after Bamber Gascoyne, the MP who defended the trade in Parliament), Bold Street (after Jonas Bold, a slave-trading merchant), elegant Georgian Rodney Street (after Admiral Rodney, a champion of the slave trade), and Seel Street (after Thomas Seel, another trader). In 1787, 37 of the 41 members of Liverpool Corporation were either slave traders or defenders of it in Parliament and, as noted above, all but one of the MPs were defenders. 'Liverpool was not just the economic capital of the slave trade,' argue Cameron and Cooke. 'It was also its political capital.' Even after abolition Liverpool continued to benefit indirectly from the institution of slavery by importing goods from the colonies where the slaves continued to work (it was only trading in slaves that had been abolished). In 1802 half of Britain's cotton imports came through Liverpool. By 1830 that proportion had reached 90 per cent.

One night at the Theatre Royal the actor George Frederick Cooke was hooted by the audience when he appeared on stage apparently drunk. Rounding on the playgoers he bawled at them: 'I have not come here to be insulted by a set of wretches [...] every brick in your infernal town is cemented with an African's blood.'

The opposition to the slave trade in Liverpool was not negligible and centred on William Roscoe, William Rathbone (member of what would become a prominent philanthropic dynasty whose fortunes were made in the timber trade, which at first supplied the builders of the slave ships), Dr Binns, Dr Currie, and James Cropper. As 'Dicky Sam', who dedicated his book on the slave trade to all these worthy gentlemen, puts it heroically, these were 'men of worth who endeavoured to raise the Negro Race to the level of man and brother, not forgetting the humble Society of Friends who were the first to condemn Slavery and to promote the Abolition of the Slave Trade'. For Dicky Sam the slave trade was 'a traffic so vile, so replete with the worst of crimes, it was the blackest stain on poor humanity'. The above were all members of the Liverpool Society for Promoting the Abolition of Slavery and they wrote pamphlets, held meetings, and defended themselves against the attacks of the merchants and traders who feared that abolition would threaten their livelihood. None of those mentioned above had any direct experience of the slave trade, but one who did was the remarkable Edward Rushton, the blind poet, revolutionary, and anti-slavery activist, who is described by his biographer, Bill Hunter, as 'a forgotten hero'.

Edward Rushton was born on 18th November 1756 in John Street. When he was not yet eleven years old, Rushton was apprenticed to a firm of West India merchants, Watt and Gregson, and by the age of 18 he was second mate in a slave ship. So appalled was the young man by the treatment meted out to the slaves on this voyage that he protested to the captain. He was accused of mutiny and threatened with being clapped in irons. Shortly after this there was an outbreak of contagious ophthalmia among the slaves – scurvy, dysentery and smallpox were other common diseases on the ships – and Rushton alone was willing to go into the hold and bring them food and water. In three weeks, Rushton succumbed to the disease and returned to Liverpool totally blind. In that condition for the next thirty years of his life he would campaign vigorously for a number of radical causes. He paid someone to read to him and studied the classics of English Literature, especially Milton, absorbing his republican spirit.

Rushton was an enthusiastic supporter of the slave revolt in San Domingo led by Toussaint L'Ouverture and in July 1796 he wrote a powerful, uncompromising letter to George Washington after he discovered that the great advocate of democracy owned slaves: 'The hypocritical bawd who preaches chastity, yet lives by the violation of it, is not truly more disgusting than one of your slave gentry bellowing in favour of democracy.' Rushton went on: 'You took arms in defence of the rights of man. Your Negroes are men. – Where, then, are the rights of your Negroes?' Washington returned the letter without answer and Rushton also received a brush-off from the great radical Tom Paine, author of the *Rights of Man* (1791).

The official opinion of the supporters of the slave trade in Liverpool was that the human traffic was 'civilising' the barbarous blacks. Thousands of pounds were spent by the local authorities in fighting the abolition movement. In 1788 the Corporation gave £100 to the Reverend Mr Harris who wrote a pamphlet, *Scriptural Researches on the Licetness of Slavery*, which demonstrated that slavery was in line with Biblical teaching and 'in conformity with the principles of natural and revealed religion delineated in the sacred writings of the work of God'. Unlike William Roscoe, who advised against any 'frontal assault' on the traders, arguing in addition that they should be compensated for loss of trade, Rushton was wholly uncompromising, possibly because he was the only Liverpool abolitionist to have direct experience of the trade. As a poet he wrote a series of 'West Indian Eclogues' in the form of exchanges between Jamaican slaves, who were given such lines as: 'Oh! for the power to make these tyrants bleed'.

The Roscoe circle preferred more moderate tactics. Even after abolition of the trade in 1807 they continued to fight the institution of slavery. James Cropper, in his *Letter...on the Injurious Effects of High Prices of Produce, and the Beneficial Effects of Low Prices on the Condition of Slaves* (1823), read to the Liverpool abolition society, argued that the current slave plantations were actually denuding the soil in the colonies by over-production, 'whilst it becomes more fertile under the hand of free men'. Abolition of slavery, he argued, would thus be in the long-term interests of masters and men: 'The friends of the cause, by thus continuing to expose, in all its native ugliness, a system alike destructive of the interests of the master and of the happiness of the slaves, and which seems to make barren the very land on which they toil, may hope to consign that system at no distant period to *universal and everlasting detestation.*' Cropper warmed to this theme and the next year in a new pamphlet claimed that converting slaves into free labourers 'will be a change nearly as advantageous, as the introduction of machinery in the spinning of cotton'.

Like many of the abolitionists, Cropper was a Quaker and a reformer – it was when the Quakers formed a special committee on the slave trade in 1783 that William Rathbone finally decided to end the supply of his family firm's timber to the slave-ship builders – and he involved himself in many other philanthropic ventures in Liverpool. His son, John, was later a friend and brother-in-law of the poet Matthew Arnold, who visited him at his house at Dingle Bank. They walked together along the banks of the Mersey on the day before Arnold's death in Liverpool. James Cropper's wealth came from Cropper, Benson, and Co.'s line of steam packets between Liverpool and America carrying mail and passengers. The atmosphere at Dingle Bank in James's day was, one observer noted, 'impregnated with holiness', and those who dined with the Croppers looked down on the plates of the dinner service to see the pleading faces of chained black slaves holding up their hands to say 'Am I not a man and a brother?' or 'Remember them that are in bonds'.

Edward Rushton did not confine his radical activities to the anti-slavery movement. Because he could no longer go to sea he was set up in a pub near the Custom House by his father, where his vocal condemnation of the press gang led to threats being made to his customers by naval officers and the consequent collapse of his trade. The press gang was something greatly feared at that time and many pubs frequented by seamen had secret tunnels which allowed them to escape if a warning came that there was a press gang in the vicinity. The anonymous author of *Liverpool A Few Years Since* (1885) describes a pre-Napoleonic press gang in Liverpool:

> At their head there was generally a rakish, dissipated, but determined-looking officer, in a very seedy uniform and shabby hat. And what followers! Fierce, savage, stern, villainous-looking fellows were they, as ready to cut a throat as eat their breakfast. What an uproar their appearance always made in the streets!

Rushton was one of the prime movers in the establishment of the Blind School in Commutation Row in 1791. In 1851 the Liverpool Blind School was purpose built and is now the Merseyside Trade Union, Community and Unemployed Resource Centre, opposite the Liverpool Philharmonic Hall. A mural inside commemorates Edward Rushton. In his letter to Washington, Rushton had declared: 'Revolutions, too [like hurricanes], for a time may produce turbulence; yet revolutions clear the political atmosphere, and contribute greatly to the comfort and happiness of the human race.' This did not, however, prevent his becoming disillusioned with the later career of Napoleon. He also took up the cause of Irish freedom and that of freedom generally, as evidenced by his poem 'The Fire of English Liberty'. In the early 1790s, to the annoyance of the authorities, he opened a bookshop in Paradise Street selling radical books.

Perhaps we should see Edward Rushton as the type of the radical defiant Scouser who is unimpressed by the claims of power. 'As children who are crammed with confectionery have no relish for plain and wholesome food,' he had told George Washington, 'so men in power, who are seldom addressed but in the sweet tones of adulation, are apt to be disgusted with the plain and salutary language of truth.' Rushton was more than ready to speak truth to power.

1 Daniel Defoe (1660?–1731), engraving by Michael van der Gucht (© Archivo Iconografico, S.A./Corbis)

2 C. G. Jung (1875–1961), 1955 (© Hulton-Deutsch Collection/Corbis)

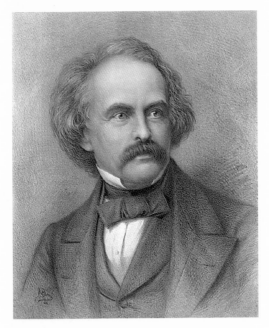

3 Nathaniel Hawthorne (1804–1864) (© Corbis)

4 Herman Melville (1819–1891) as a young man, painted by Asa W. Twitchell (© Bettmann/Corbis)

5 The Folly, Folly Lane, now Islington, demolished c. 1785, painted by W. G. Herdman (1843) (LVRO)

6 Welsh Presbyterian Church, 1868, painted by W. G. Herdman (LVRO)

7 Interior of the Liverpool Islamic Institute and Mosque, Brougham Terrace, 1899 (LVRO)

8 The Herculaneum Pottery in an engraving from an 1806 share certificate (NML archive)

9 William Roscoe (1753–1831) (LVRO)

10 Alexis de Tocqueville (1805–1859) (© Stefano Bianchetti/Corbis)

11 St George's Hall, c. 1870, painted by Glyn Morris (LVRO)

12 Walker Art Gallery, 1895 (LVRO)

13 Robert Southey (1774–1843) (© Bettmann/Corbis)

14 Thomas de Quincey (1785–1859) (© Bettmann/Corbis)

15 Jesse Hartley (1780–1860), surveyor to the Liverpool Dock Trustees (LVRO)

16 Albert Dock, c. 1920 (LVRO)

17 J. A. Picton, architect and historian, and founder of the Liverpool Free Library (LVRO)

18 Dr William Henry Duncan (1805–1863), Liverpool's first Medical Officer of Health (LVRO)

19 Liverpool Workhouse, Brownlow Hill, c. 1925 (LVRO)

20 Court housing in Bostock Street, c. 1900 (LVRO)

21 T. P. O'Connor (1848–1929), MP for Scotland Division (LVRO)

22 Matthew Arnold (1822–1888) (© Bettmann/Corbis)

23 Statue of Hugh Stowell Brown (1823–1886), Baptist preacher and social reformer, in front of the Baptist church, Myrtle Street, 1921

6

Christian Politeness

I can still see him. I shall always still see him. He does not haunt me. I am not traumatised by him. Perhaps, if he were still alive, I could come to pity him. But for now he serves a purpose. He is a symbol of power, its dejected arrogance, and how easily it is abused. I am grateful to him for teaching me a very simple and strong lesson which I have never forgotten: *I am not on the same side as people like you*. What better lesson in life could I have been taught?

We were in the school gym when he appeared at the door and called out my name. I followed him to the smelly changing-room where he proceeded to offer me an interesting choice: six strokes of the strap with my trousers up or four with them down. Brother Francis, headmaster of the school, was a small man but into his tiny frame he packed a great deal of pent anger and vindictive energy. Behind his thick lenses those tiny, fierce eyes flamed aggressively, his face was tomato-red, his lips pursed tightly now in an unsavoury grimace.

Before administering the sentence he issued another rebuke. My place in class had fallen virtually to the bottom. I was a disreputable pupil. At this I managed a terrified squeak of protest. I had actually gone up several places, though I had never been and never would be top of any class or list. A spasm of distaste shot through his features as he looked down at the register in his left hand. He had made a mistake. It was my namesake, George Murray, he was after. Curtly and contemptuously he dismissed me with an instruction to send in poor George. I walked back to the gym, pushing open the door in triumph to acknowledge the looks of my mates. The gym-master, like all his fellow-teachers, did not wish to know what had been going on, and looked away uncomfortably. With a dismissive nod he allowed me to pass on the message to George. I resumed my business on the wall-bars.

There was nothing particularly unusual about this incident. Over a number of years now (I suppose I was twelve or thirteen at the time) I had grown used to this sort of thing. I had come to associate men in dog-collars with acts of casual violence. It was a school addicted to it. Regular strappings – sometimes twenty pupils at a time, lined up in a row – cuffings, the head slammed down from behind against the desk followed by profuse bleeding from the nose. This latter happened to me at least twice and I wasn't one of the especially naughty ones. Rough, hard treatment, to boys who were not the roughest in a tough city by any means. After all, we lived in one of the milder, lower-middle-class suburbs.

We have been inundated in recent years with accounts of the misdemeanours of the Irish Christian Brothers. And there is much truth in the claim that more than a dash of anti-Irish racism lurks in some of the gloating at the Catholic Church's discomfort. There is no reason for anyone to be retroactively vindictive, and I myself don't feel particularly damaged by it. In fact, I now see that the experience above taught me a moral and political lesson that has served me so well in life that I must in all honesty acknowledge a debt to that angry, red-faced, nasty little man. Instead of being angry, now, I feel only a little sad and perhaps sorry for these lonely, maladjusted men. No sympathy whatsover of course for the dishonest hierarchies with their contemptible cover-ups and none for those who went further: the sexual abusers whom, mercifully, I never encountered.

The film-maker Terence Davies, whose (for me) heart-rending first film, *Children*, based on his experiences at the Sacred Heart boys' school in Liverpool, together with his more ambitious later films of the 1980s and 1990s, *Distant Voices, Still Lives* and *The Long Day Closes*, constitute the most profoundly moving accounts of post-war Liverpool Catholic culture, writes in the introduction to the collected screenplays of his purpose in making them:

> The reason I began making films came from a deep *need* to do so in order to come to terms with my family's history and suffering, to make sense of the past and to explore my own personal terrors, both mental and spiritual, and to examine the destructive nature of Catholicism. Film as an expression of guilt, film as confession (psychotherapy would be much cheaper but a lot less fun).

Davies' words will find an echo with many Liverpudlians who have come, as I did, through similar experiences (we are almost of the same generation): the prevailing sense that one had gone through some sort of experience that needed 'coming to terms with', the sense of inherited family traditions, of the collective memory of past privations and sufferings, of the need to explore those 'personal terrors' that had, for some reason, been implanted and stirred up in young boys and girls. It is quite an inheritance and even those of us who hope that we are not 'screwed up' feel that we are carrying a great deal of baggage and are not entirely sure why it was considered necessary to be loaded down with it. Plainly there are those – and there are many of them in Liverpool, still worshipping in the churches where congregations are shrinking week by week, and where young men are no longer coming forward in sufficient numbers to staff them and embrace the celibate life – who do not share Davies' conviction about the 'destructive nature of Catholicism'. And I wonder if our European contemporaries – French, Italian, Spanish – would report quite the same level of comprehensive foul-up that English and Irish Catholics seem to take for granted – at least the disenchanted ones.

I grew up in Liverpool as what the newspapers always call a 'devout' Catholic. We were scrupulous in our observance, never missing the weekly Mass, even on holiday, fasting, eating fish on Friday (it was only the way fish was cooked in those days that made this seem like a penance, if that is what it was intended to be – a plate of lightly grilled sea-bass washed down with a glass of chardonnay would seem one of the lighter acts of self-denial), going to confession where we racked our brains for something sinful enough to confess. My own father had spent his childhood and adolescence in Catholic seminaries at Upholland in Lancashire (where he sometimes only just got enough to eat) and eventually at the English College in Rome, where he finally decided that he did not have a vocation and returned, the former poor boy from Bootle, with fluent Italian and a knowledge of Latin and Greek. In hospital recovering from an illness in later life he exchanged witty letters in Latin with an aged priest in a neighbouring ward.

When, on another occasion, my father had a bout of flu my mother was instructed to bring news of the election of the latest Pope. I was in another room doing my homework when my mother came from the kitchen, where she had been listening to the news on the wireless, to the bottom of the stairs

58

to shout up 'Montini!' The College of Cardinals had sent up their white smoke and chosen Cardinal Montini as the next Pope Paul VI. I had a cousin who was a Montfort Father and an aunt who was a Sister of Charity of the order of St Vincent de Paul, with a great flowering bonnet which shrank over the years in wave after wave of modernisation until in the end it was hardly noticeable. The strict rules of her order prevented her from eating a meal in the home of any of her relatives so we would sometimes meet her in other people's houses. One day I carried a tray of tea and biscuits out to her in the public Marine Gardens in front of our house. Sadly, at the end, her mind went and my last memory of her is at a family occasion, at the far end of the room, raising a tot of gin with happy, vacant eyes and declaring 'We're all Holy Joes over here.'

I myself was an altar boy, getting up in the dark and cold to go to the early Mass and sing out the Latin responses. I can still plainchant large sections of the Nicene Creed in Latin to myself while waiting for a bus. I remember church processions in the springtime when we cast flower petals on the ground. I remember also the contingent of the Catholic Young Men's Society, marching behind their banner. The CYMS (pronounced 'See Why Mess') always raised a chuckle because many of its hobbling oldsters were plainly sailing under false colours.

Destructive? Not I think in my case, but it is something that one carries with one, even after the abandonment of one's faith, a permanent cluster of feelings and memories. I would hate it if it were a freemasonry, a secret sodality, but when I meet other Catholics – who generally turn out to be ex-Catholics – I never feel that it is. I don't want to be interpreted by my badge. The principal legacy is what conventional wisdom says it is, an obsessive refinement of conscience ('Catholic guilt'), that sense that one is almost certainly a sinner in every case and that if a misdemeanour has been committed in the vicinity then one is probably a legitimate suspect. The Puritan who abhors sin, is wholly free from it, touched by providential grace and saved, points, in a spasm of horrified self-righteousness, to the sinner on the other side of the street. He is pointing at me.

I have nobody left to point to.

At my Christian Brothers' school, there was a curious survival, a small textbook called *Christian Politeness* which I cannot believe is any longer in use anywhere. I have a dim memory of it, but a slightly more vivid recollection of the call, during lessons of religious instruction: 'Get out your *Christian Politeness!*' I called one up from the bowels of the British Library. First published in 1862, *The Rules of Christian Politeness* was issued in an English translation (the author the Venerable De La Salle, founder of an order himself) by Mrs J. Sadleir in Dublin, a little book hardly larger than a packet of slim cigars, that could be slipped into a breast pocket. It is divided into two sections: 'On the Modesty which Ought to Appear in the Exterior' and 'On Propriety in Common and Ordinary Actions'. I wonder which section Brother Francis was using as his guide that morning in the changing room?

Some of the book's strictures seem quite sensible enough ('Children are guilty of unpardonable rudeness when they spit in the face of a companion; neither are they excusable who spit from windows, or on the walls or furniture'). I have no probem with that. It even gives useful advice on what to do if you are an ugly bastard: 'They to whom nature has denied the advantage of a pleasing aspect, should try to diminish, as far as possible, their natural infirmity, and endeavour to assume a more cheerful and a more agreeable countenance.' And, quite naturally in a Christian Brothers' school, there is a scrupulous attention to exact sexual propriety: 'When clothing our body, we ought to remember that it bears the imprint of sin; we ought, therefore, to cover it with decency, in accordance with the law of God.'

I take this to mean that I should have gone for the six-with-the-trousers-up option.

The chapter on food and diet pronounces that '[all] conversation relating to affairs of the table should likewise be forbidden... never speaking with an air of satisfaction of any repasts, no matter how good they may have been'. At a time when the English middle classes appear to speak of little else than 'affairs of the table' this rule doesn't have much of a future. And, finally, a rule that is terrible in its implications for Liverpudlians in general and this Liverpudlian in particular: 'we are allowed to laugh and to be merry, for the Wise Man tells us that there is a time for laughing. But laughter ought always to be moderate; to laugh very loudly is rudeness; to laugh without a cause is folly; to laugh at every little incident that occurs is levity and giddiness.' *To laugh without a cause is folly.* Oh, bless me, Father, for I have sinned!

I have just quoted, for those not familiar with the ritual, the words that Catholics use in the confessional. I always liked the idea of confession, its frank admission that we are all sinners and are likely to remain so for the duration. I loved the delightful idea that we could have a brief holiday before starting all over again on the muddy path of sin. I think that this intellectual motion has stayed with me for ever: the clean sheet, the new chapter, the morning resolution, the emptied drawer, the box of rubbish packed ready for the tip, are all symptoms of a belief that we can scratch out the mistakes we have made and start again, just like that. The problem was that, especially as children, we could never quite decide what to propose as evidence of our sinfulness. The invisible man behind the grille was probably expecting something meaty but all our sins were pretty trivial. We suspected that sexual misdemeanours or 'impure thoughts' were the best bet and certain verbal formulas were available that allowed us to strike a balance between sufficient indication and elegant avoidance. As Anthony Kenny, the Oxford philosopher who was a curate in Liverpool at the end of the 1950s, put it very wisely in his autobiography, *A Path From Rome* (1986): 'Interestingly wicked people never go to confession at all; most of those who go do not realize what their real sins are.'

In December 1850 the Reverend John Conor, incumbent of St Simon's parish in Liverpool, delivered a speech to the Church Pastoral Aid Society in Hull intended to make his audience feel grateful at having escaped the sinful toxicity of Liverpool. There was, as we shall see later, a flourishing genre in the nineteenth century of religious commentary on the state of the Liverpool poor and Conor was merely one of the more colourful practitioners. 'Every twentieth house [in the parish] was a beer shop, or spirit vault,' he thundered, 'and above the door of every tenth was written, "this way to hell going down to the chambers of death".' Six thousand wretched people were squeezed into 21 streets and 68 courts in a fifteen-acre plot of ground in St Simon's parish which the cleric called 'this moral wilderness'. Moving on from the usual indictments – booze and general fecklessness – he identified one of the most potent causes of the people's misery: Popery. Fulminating against 'the Babylonish hosts of Priests, Sisters of False Charity, and miscalled Christian Brothers', Conor held up to his awe-struck audience his collection of 'Roman trumpery', including a rosary and a miraculous medal.

As a child I had at least one miraculous medal, made of a papery light grey alloy and showing, if my recall is correct, the open-handed gesture of the typical image of the Virgin. I don't think we were particularly superstitious or credulous in my family but in a glass case in the front room reserved for visitors and Christmas parties there was a bottle of Lourdes water that someone more pious than we were had brought back from the shrine. As a small child, with a painful cut finger, I once went to the case and took out the bottle, which stood next to a tiny model of one of the Swiss Guards that protect the Pope in the Vatican. I dabbed a few drops on the wound but absolutely nothing happened. My scepticism was making an early start. At around this time, however, I was given a book called *Saints and Heroes* bound in yellow boards. I cannot now remember all the names of those exemplary figures but I do know that St Francis was one of them and that he became my hero because he loved animals. More to the point, when you passed savage dogs on the walk to school, all you needed to do was to say a silent prayer to St Francis, and they would leave you alone. I can testify to the complete success of this intercession. My dismembered flesh, torn apart by those sharp fangs, was never scattered across the lawns of Moorside Park and I reached school intact every time.

Today we joke about such things, but in the sixteenth century, Catholicism in Liverpool and in the Lancashire countryside was no laughing matter. The state repression of believers was comprehensive and savage in its violence. Within months of the accession of Queen Elizabeth all the English bishops were imprisoned for life and the Mass was proscribed so absolutely that anybody convicted of being a priest or harbouring one would be sentenced to be hanged and then cut down and chopped into small pieces while still alive. The ferocity of the Tudor repressions is something we don't tend to think about these days. It doesn't fit our national myth of ourselves: after all it was the other lot that ran the Inquisition, wasn't it? The gentle, moderate, rather wet English with their sensible shoes firmly placed on the *via media* couldn't possibly have burnt someone's intestines in front of their face. Could they?

At the start of the persecutions of Catholics there were probably about fifty secret chapels within two hours' horse ride of Liverpool, mostly in the halls of the local landed gentry, where a disguised priest was either being concealed or a regular visitor. Robert Stonor, in his *Liverpool's Hidden Story* (1957), talks of 'this prolonged drama of hide-and-seek between disguised priests and government spies, with little boats slipping across the Mersey by night, and sliding panels masking secret rooms behind oak wainscoting'.

As a child I grew up with a sense of some of this, and of the historic example of 'the English Martyrs'. We knew about priests' hiding holes and sang an extraordinarily rousing hymn, 'Faith of our fathers, holy faith/We will be true to thee till death', but I don't think we wallowed in propaganda. By the time I was at school the old sectarian conflicts and battles – which once rivalled the ferocity of those in Belfast – were over. Just north of where I lived was a hamlet called Little Crosby where every single resident was said to be a Catholic. We all believed this but I don't quite see how it could have been enforced and it doesn't sound very desirable. The local family, the Blundells of Crosby, had defended their ancient faith for centuries and left copious records, the most famous being the great diary or 'Diurnall' of Nicholas Blundell (1669–1737). Earlier, Richard Blundell was one of the first Catholics to be arrested, in 1568, as a shelterer of priests and the family was subjected to constant arrests and house searchings.

In 1609 the Rector of Sefton, Gregory Turner, refused to bury the body of a poor Catholic woman, Jane Harvey of Ince Blundell, because of her religion. Her friends buried her near the roadside cross in Cross Lane. That night a pig grubbing for food dug up her body and ate half of the corpse. William Blundell was so incensed at this that he enclosed a piece of ground called the Harkirke as a place for those refused burial. I used to cycle past the Harkirke as a child and it was said to have been the site of a Saxon church where 300 Saxon coins had been dug up during a Danish raid in 913. William Blundell had the coins melted down and made into a chalice which survived until the 1950s when it was stolen. The authorities were outraged by the construction of the Harkirke burial ground and William was summoned to the Star Chamber and finded £2000. Nevertheless, 105 lay people and 26 priests were subsequently buried at the Harkirke. The burials were done at night when nobody was about because the penalty for sheltering a priest was to be hanged, drawn and quartered. On one occasion the High Sheriff had the gravestones destroyed and the crosses carried away. As William's daughter, a nun in Louvain (the Blundells had a fearful number of nuns in the family) expressed it, this action 'was done with sound of trumpet, they both coming and going away with great pomp'.

The Blundells found themselves again on the wrong side of the religious fence at the Civil War when a later William Blundell had his whole estate sequestered by the Parliamentarians. Nicholas Blundell's diary recorded that after the Jacobite invasion of 1715 and the subsequent reaction the house was once again searched 'by some Foot'. But at the time of writing there are still Blundells at Little Crosby. Robert Stonor calls the family 'the god-parents of the present day Catholic Liverpool'. Pious Catholics like my parents had a great deal of esteem for the Blundells and when they came to find a name for their eldest son – only a couple of years after the latest Nicholas Blundell had died prematurely at the age of 24 – I think they may have been influenced by this in their choice of name.

But St Nicholas was also patron saint of sailors and the sea. And wasn't that also the name of the only English Pope?

7

The Bootle Cow

As the grandson of a *fin-de-siècle* Bootle barber, I generally feel obliged to come to the defence of that particular patch of north Liverpool. But a district (no longer, to the injury of its municipal pride, a separate County Borough with its own police force as it was in my childhood) whose name rhymes most readily with words such as pootle, footle, tootle and rootle presents certain difficulties. Lawrence Murray (1875–1918) learned his hairdressing trade at the Albany salon in the city centre but set up eventually on his own at 202 Knowsley Road, Bootle. The kids used to play Grand National in the empty shop after hours, blowing little pieces of paper representing horses along the long bench, worn smooth by countless Bootle backsides waiting for their owners' chins to be shaved. After his death from TB in 1918 the goodwill of the shop was sold to a gloomy Scot called MacPherson who eventually threw himself over the rail of the Irish Boat, his corpse subsequently washing up on the foreshore at Seaforth. Lawrence was a socialist who read Robert Blatchford's *Clarion* newspaper and liked to tuck up his white apron and pootle off for a pint at lunchtime at a pub called

The Ship, where a sign still swings showing a Cunard liner sailing at full speed ahead.

Lying awake at night I used to hear the low, melancholy booming of the foghorn out on the river known as the Bootle Cow. I think I can still hear it in my dreams. Many of Bootle's streets had been named after Oxford colleges and many after poets. Cowper Street was not pronounced as it would have been at the High Table at St John's, and Balliol Road Baths, where I learned to swim, was pronounced not as Baylliol and Barths but with those two 'a's flat and hard as a barber's strop. Bootle in the late eighteenth century and early nineteenth century was, it seems, a pastoral spot. 'I have seen wild roses growing upon the very ground that is now the centre of Bootle', William Gladstone recalled in his autobiography. And the shipping magnate William Forwood also remembered the 'sylvan retreats' of Marsh Lane. By the time my father was born there in 1913 this would not have been the first impression it created. Today, it is probably best known – though it would sincerely wish not to be – for something far more tragic.

On Friday 12th February 1993 a young Bootle mother was queueing for meat in a butcher's shop at the Strand Shopping Centre in Stanley Road, Bootle, when she looked down and saw that her two-year-old son, James, was not at her side. An immediate police search was started but all too quickly the body of the young boy, a month short of his third birthday, was found on a railway track at Walton, brutally murdered. It would turn out that his killers were two young boys who had lured him away to the railway embankment. The smudgy CCTV footage of James Bulger being led away by the two boys at 15:42:32 on 12th February 1993 (by some pointless irony the camera was that of the Mothercare store) was imprinted on the consciousness of the nation and not just that of shocked Liverpudlians. At Liverpool's home football match at Anfield against Ipswich Town the next Saturday 35,000 fans observed a minute's silence. On the Kop a banner was raised reading: R.I.P. JAMES. It was a shocking murder, disturbingly gratuitous and without motive, but one that could have happened anywhere. Bootle is no more violent than any other urban area of Britain, yet there were some in the media who were biting their tongues at the spectacle of Liverpool grieving again. Four years earlier, when the Hillsborough football disaster occurred, on 15 April 1989, one of the leading British tabloid newspapers, the *Sun*, owned by Rupert Murdoch, accused the Liverpool fans of stealing from the dead bodies and urinating on corpses, an unfounded allegation for which, ten years later, the newspaper publicly apologised. But its sales in Liverpool have never recovered. One headline at the time of Hillsborough hit home. Liverpool was branded by another Murdoch title, *The Sunday Times*, as 'Self-pity City'.

For those of us in the great Scouse diaspora (300,000 people left Liverpool during the 1970s and 1980s and I was one of them) something very disturbing was happening. The traditional image of the jokey, irreverent Liverpudlian was being replaced by a completely different image which we couldn't recognise: a whining, lachrymose sentimentalist with an over-developed sense of grievance. It seemed that when someone in Littlehampton tripped on a banana skin they picked themselves up and carried on walking; when the same thing happened in Liverpool it was seen as the latest act of a vengeful God smiting the Scouser in his affliction. In part this was just the usual tabloid nonsense, in part it was a misreading of Scouse semiotics: the affronted tone, the playing-up, have always been part of the act and shouldn't have been taken so seriously. But underneath something real was going on. Liverpool was, it seemed, disproportionately suffering from unemployment and recession during the

Thatcher years. Alan Bleasdale's Yosser Hughes, as we have seen, touched a raw nerve. Liverpool felt let down or just plain confused at the direction in which it was heading – or apparently wasn't heading. All that has now changed. The decline of population has been reversed, unemployment is low, new jobs are being created, the exiles are trickling back, the world is handing out its baubles – the city has now been declared by UNESCO a World Heritage Site and, yes, in 2008 it is to be the European Capital of Culture – and the negative jokes about fecklessness and thievery ('What do you call a Scouser in a suit? The Accused') are beginning to seem a bit old hat. The 1980s were a bad period for Liverpool and for its reputation, but they are over. The last blast on this particular plastic trumpet was the penitential visit by the editor of the *Spectator*, Boris Johnson, in 2004, to Liverpool to apologise for having yet again given vent to the self-pity calumny.

I thought of the Bootle Cow again when I re-read Herman Melville's Liverpool novel, *Redburn* (1849). In his fictionalised account of his arrival at Liverpool on 4th July 1839 in fog and mist and grey dawn, the great novelist was 'startled by the doleful, dismal sound of a great bell, whose slow intermittent tolling sounded in unison with the solemn roll of the billows'. That wasn't my siren-like booming cry in the night but it sounds just as lowering to the spirits and conducive to burying your head under the bedcovers with a book and a torch.

Melville had set sail on the *St Lawrence* from a wharf at the bottom of Wall Street at the age of nineteen. Captain Brown's 'coppered and copper-fastened' 500-ton vessel – carrying bales of cotton and passengers – carried Melville as a greenhorn boy on his first voyage and, arriving on Independence Day in Liverpool Bay, the ship was greeted by a patriotic display from all the American ships in the port. Yet when the *St Lawrence* finally anchored in the river, Melville was disappointed by what he saw:

> Looking shoreward, I beheld lofty ranges of dingy ware-houses, which seemed very deficient in the elements of the marvelous; and bore a most unexpected resemblance to the ware-houses along South-street in New York. There was nothing strange; nothing extraordinary about them... To be sure, I did not expect that every house in Liverpool must be a Leaning Tower of Pisa, or a Strasbourg Cathedral; but yet, these edifices I must confess, were a sad and bitter disappointment to me.

Eventually the ship found a berth and the pilot guided them into the Prince's Dock where the *St Lawrence* lay for the next six weeks. Disembarking, Melville and several of his fellow-sailors set off for a lodging house called the Baltimore Clipper, where he could reflect at last that he was now 'seated upon an English bench, under an English roof, in an English tavern, forming an integral part of the English empire'. But there was something else about Liverpool that Melville – or his fictional counterpart, Wellingborough Redburn – was about to discover:

> of all seaports in the world, Liverpool, perhaps, most abounds in all the variety of land-sharks, land-rats, and other vermin, which make the hapless mariner their prey. In the shape of landlords, bar-keepers, clothiers, crimps, and boarding-house loungers, the land-sharks devour him, limb by limb; while the land-rats and mice constantly nibble at his purse.

Liverpool, in short, was expert at fleecing the incoming sailor, particularly the foreign one. 'And yet,' Melville went on, 'sailors love this Liverpool; and upon long voyages to distant parts of the globe, will be continually dilating on its charms and attractions, and extolling it above all other seaports in the world. For in Liverpool they find their Paradise – not the well known street of that name – and one of them told me he would be content to lie in Prince's Dock till he *hove up anchor* for the world to come.'

As Melville began to explore Liverpool he carried with him a book of his father's called *The Picture of Liverpool* (1803), 'bound in green morocco'. He noted a reference in it to a request made by the citizens to Queen Elizabeth in 1571 for relief of a tax imposed on 'her Majesty's poor decayed town of Liverpool' and could not help contrasting that epithet with the port's visible buoyancy and commercial boom-town feeling. The population of Liverpool had doubled in the first thirty years of the nineteenth century and four years before Melville's arrival Alexis de Tocqueville, in his *Journey to England* (1835), pronounced that Liverpool was a town 'destined to become the centre of English trade'. He was prob-ably one of the last to declare 'Liverpool is a beautiful town', adding: 'Poverty is almost as great as it is at Manchester, but it is hidden. Fifty thousand poor people live in cellars. Sixty thousand Irish Catholics.' De Tocqueville quizzed the French consul about a range of commercial matters, especially French wine imports, and put it to him: 'Liverpool is growing the whole time?', to which the consul replied: 'Incredibly fast. Everything goes at a run. The railway will further speed up the rate at which London can be by-passed as a seaport.'

One of the last visitors to the less frantic Liverpool of the late eighteenth and early nineteenth century was Thomas de Quincey, author of *The Confessions of an English Opium-Eater*. In the summer of 1801 he spent his summer holidays at Everton where his mother had rented a cottage in Middle Lane (now Everton Terrace). Everton, according to de Quincey's biographer, Grevel Lindop (another exiled Liverpudlian), was at this time 'a delightful country village, built on the slopes of a hill overlooking Liverpool Bay, famous for good sea-air and a popular site for the holiday villas of the well-to-do'. It is inconceivable that anyone today would think of holidaying in Everton, pleasant as its wide streets and elevated position still are for the urban stroller. At the mansion of the local banker, William Clarke, de Quincey met William Roscoe (1753–1831), one of Liverpool's most famous indigenous figures. Roscoe is summed up by his biographer, George Chandler:

> He was Liverpool's cultural pioneer *par excellence*, and there is hardly any movement or institution in modern Liverpool which does not owe some part of its existence or tradition to his work... Look at his record: first well-known Liverpool poet; organiser of the first art exhibition of its kind in Liverpool; leader of the movement against the slave trade (although this was believed to be the foundation of Liverpool's prosperity); successful lawyer and banker; writer of idealistic political songs which swept the country; historian of world reputation; Member of Parliament; connoisseur and collector of international significance; one of the earliest writers of poems for children, some of which are classics; author of a book of botany which is still a collector's piece; advocate of prison reform and political freedom; patron of fine printing of quite outstanding beauty; devout Christian who would not abate one jot of his beliefs as a dissenter to secure preferment.

De Quincey, however, could not let this dazzling inventory of virtues and accomplishments interfere with his literary judgement, finding Roscoe's poetry full of 'the most timid and blind servility to the narrowest of conventional usages, conventional ways of viewing things, conventional forms of expression'. De Quincey was already aware, in 1801, of the poetic revolution being launched by Wordsworth that would sweep away the polished but empty facility of men like Roscoe, and create 'a new birth in poetry'. He wrote: 'It was secretly amusing to contrast the little artificial usages of their petty traditional knack [i.e. that of Roscoe and his circle] with the natural forms of a divine art – the difference being pretty much as between an American lake, Ontario or Superior, and a carp pond or a tench preserve'. In other words, Roscoe was a provincial. A more sympathetic picture is painted by the poet Robert Southey the following summer in his *Letters from England*. Southey praised Roscoe's pioneering life of Lorenzo de Medici 'which even the Italians have thought worthy of translation' and claimed that the people of Liverpool at the turn of the century were proud of their townsman: 'whether they read his book or not, they are sensible it has reflected honour upon their town in the eyes of England and of Europe... This high and just estimation of Mr Roscoe is the more praiseworthy, because he is known to be an enemy to the slave trade, the peculiar disgrace of Liverpool.'

Perhaps the most significant legacy of Roscoe today in Liverpool is the bequest of his collection of early Italian art (he never actually visited Italy) to the city, which eventually became the nucleus of the collection of the Walker Art Gallery. I can forgive any number of those dreary auto-pilot Augustan couplets for the gift of the most beautiful painting in the Walker, attributed to Lukas Cranach the Elder, *The Nymph of the Fountain* (1534). The Walker is the biggest municipal art gallery in England and I spent many hours there in my childhood and adolescence. I was haunted by Lucian Freud's *Interior in Paddington*, painted in 1951, the year before I was born, and commissioned for the Festival of Britain. The painting continues to startle me every time I come upon it again. Its subject, Harry Diamond, was a friend of Freud's, a scene-shifter and odd-job man who became a photographer in the

1960s. He visited Liverpool in 1979 and told the staff of the Walker Art Gallery that he had been required to stand for this picture over a period of six months. I also loved another painting, which used to be called *A Disputed Bill of Costs* (now restored to its original title *A Visit to a Lawyer's Office*). A not especially distinguished Victorian narrative painting, it shows a whiskered man and his son who have been made to wait in a lawyer's office while the whispering clerks on the other side of a wooden partition decide what to do about the challenge to the bill. It was partly the picture and partly its title that intrigued me as a child. And there were plenty of Pre-Raphaelites which I found (and have secretly continued to find) rather dreamy and insipid.

On that July day in 1802, Southey made the observation that '[there] is no cathedral, no castle, gate, town wall, or monument of antiquity, no marks of decay. Everything is the work of late years, almost of the present generation'. Nineteenth-century Liverpool continued this work of laying waste to most of its eighteenth-century buildings in the rush to expand and exploit every inch of space for commercial purposes. But the traditions of civic patronage were upheld. 'Fortunes are made here with a rapidity unexampled in any other part of England,' Southey noted, but added: 'There is too a princely liberality in its merchants, which even in London is not rivalled.' He instanced the endowment of the Botanic Garden and the Athenaeum. A similar point was made in 1807 by James Stonehouse in his *The Stranger in Liverpool* that Liverpool had 'no valued remains of ancient, barbarous, or classic architecture', which meant that its history 'is the history of the silent, but powerful, operations of industry'.

By the time of Melville's arrival thirty years later dock-building had surged forward. The first wet dock to be built in Liverpool – docks being vital to counter the disadvantages of the Mersey estuary in terms of wind, currents, sandbanks, and tidal range – was Thomas Steers' Old Dock, opened in 1715. But the real boom in dock-building was in the first half of the nineteenth century, and the greatest dock-builder was the Pontefract engineer Jesse Hartley (1780–1860), responsible for today's most impressive refurbished structure, the Albert Dock. The Prince's Dock, where Melville's ship berthed, was completed only in 1821, which meant that much of the dock architecture he saw would have been relatively new. He was impressed: 'I never tired of admiring them'. Previously, he had seen 'only the miserable wooden wharves, and slip-shod, shambling piers of New York', with the result that 'the sight of these mighty docks filled my young mind with wonder and delight'. New York's untidy and straggling wharves, Melville considered, were a disgrace to the city:

> Whereas, in Liverpool, I beheld long China walls of masonry, vast piers of stone; and a succession of granite-rimmed docks, completely inclosed, and many of them communicating, which almost recalled to mind the great American chain of lakes: Ontario, Erie, St. Clair, Huron, Michigan and Superior. The extent and solidity of these structures, seemed equal to what I had read of the old Pyramids of Egypt... For miles you may walk along that river-side, passing dock after dock, like a chain of immense fortresses: – Prince's, George's, Salt-House, Clarence, Brunswick, Trafalgar, King's, Queen's, and many more.

Melville was impressed at how each dock was a kind of 'walled town, full of life and commotion', with ships from every part of the globe jostling together 'as in a grand parliament of masts' in an intimacy in which 'yard-arm touches yard-arm in brotherly love'. It made each Liverpool dock 'a grand caravansary inn'.

As a child I loved to watch the ships coming in and out

of the port from the front window of our house at Waterloo, with binoculars trained on the ships and a publication on my knee that pictured all the funnels against the names of the shipping lines to which they belonged – the chequered pattern of the Ellerman Lines, the yellow (if I recall correctly) of the Elder Dempster 'banana boats', the blue and black of the Blue Funnel lines with their classical names such as *Hector* and *Ajax*. One of my treasured possessions is a copy of Walter Pater's *The Renaissance* picked up in a Liverpool secondhand bookshop. Its cover is stamped in gilt with the words THE BLUE FUNNEL LINE LIBRARY and, number 51 in that library, it bears the additional gilt name of 'T.S.S. Hector'. On Friday nights the magnificent white Canadian Pacific transatlantic liners sailed out on the tide, giving a huge hoot as they passed as if it were addressed to us personally. These days, as one swings out into the Mersey on the ferry ('Welcome to the most famous ferry in the world', begins the recorded patter modestly), there isn't, frankly, much shipping about, except for the Belfast and Dublin ferries which seem to be run by Scandinavians to judge from their names, *Mersey Viking* and the 'Norsemerchant.com' in big white letters on the side of the hull. I doubt if you could now buy my ship spotter's guide which used to be available in all the newsagents. Sometimes I would cycle all the way to the kiosk at the Gladstone Dock at Seaforth on a Saturday morning to get a copy of the *Journal of Commerce* which listed the day's sailings.

In Melville's day and earlier there would have been much more excitement on the river, created by the need for the sailing ships to wait for the wind, rather than being sedately pulled out by tugs and the engines started. Here is Henry Smithers in his *Liverpool, its Commerce, Statistics and Institutions* (1825) on the sudden excitement when the winds were judged right:

Some little time before high water the dock-gates are thrown open; the utmost alacrity is seen to prevail on every side, each vessel striving first to pass through. The authoritative voice of the dock master, issuing his mandates, is heard above all other sounds; captains pressing forward to their stations, passengers with their luggage, market-carts with provisions for the vessels, all are in motion; boats are seen passing to and fro, the river is crowded with ships preparing for sea, whilst beloved friends press to the pier-head to wave a last adieu and offer up their orisons for a prosperous voyage; the whole resembling the activity and enjoyment of a hive of bees in the first warm days of spring.

Or the pseudonymous 'Old Stager' of *Liverpool A Few Years Since* (1885):

There were no steamers in those days to tow out our vessels. The wind ruled supreme, without a rival. The consequence was, that when, after a long stretch of contrary winds, a change took place, and a favourable breeze set in, a whole fleet of ships would at once be hauled out of dock, and start upon their several voyages. It was a glorious spectacle.

At around the same time, Robert Southey was at the waterfront: 'Two ships came in while we were upon the quay: it was a beautiful sight to see them enter the docks and take their quiet station, a crowd flocking towards them, some in curiosity to know what they were, others in hope and fear, hastening to see who had returned in them.' As the nineteenth century progressed the steamers would replace this silent beauty with the throb of screws.

8

The Wild Irish

As he continued his 'roving' through the streets of Liverpool during that summer of 1839, Melville came into direct contact with the great, unavoidable reality of nineteenth-century Liverpool: mass poverty:

> I used to crowd my way through masses of squalid men, women, and children, who at this evening hour, in those quarters of Liverpool, seem to empty themselves into the street, and live there for the time. I had never seen any thing like it in New York... In these haunts, beggary went on before me wherever I walked, and dogged me unceasingly at the heels. Poverty, poverty, poverty, in almost endless vistas: and want and woe staggered arm in arm along these miserable streets.

A particular incident was engraved on Melville's memory and fictionalised in *Redburn*. The eponymous hero of the novel passed each day, on his way to his lodgings at the Baltimore Clipper in Union Street, through a narrow street lined with cotton warehouses near the docks, called Launcelott's Hey. One day he heard a 'soul-sickening wail' coming from a gloomy cellar some fifteen feet below one of the warehouses and, looking down, saw 'the figure of what had been a woman. Her blue arms folded to her livid bosom two shrunken things like children, that leaned toward her, one on each side.' They were 'next to dead with want' and had crawled into this cellar, he was convinced, in order to die. So shocked was Melville by the sight that he accosted two old women who were scrounging nearby in the rubbish for bits of discarded cotton which they would wash and sell for next to nothing. They had no sympathy for the starving woman and her children, nor did a passing policeman who told him as a Yankee to mind his own business. It was the same story back at his lodgings. There was little scope for charity among people who were themselves in want. Eventually he found some bread and cheese and some water and took it down to the cellar, where he was shocked to discover that the woman was clutching to herself a dead baby. He began to wonder if he had made a mistake in bringing them food, 'for it would only tend to prolong their misery, without hope of any permanent relief: for die they must very soon'. So desperate was their predicament that the thought even came to him that he would be doing them a service if he could find some way of 'putting an end to their horrible lives'. For the next two days he dropped off some bread for them but on the third day they had vanished: 'In place of the woman and children, a heap of quick-lime was glistening'.

What Melville observed had taken place in a city where merchants and shipowners had grown rich. According to historian Tony Lane in *Liverpool: Gateway of Empire* (1987), 'Liverpool produced more wealthy families in the nineteenth century than any other English city... from 1804 to 1914, Merseyside produced almost twice as many millionaires as Greater Manchester and, outside London, was only surpassed by Clydeside'. Throughout the century the contrast between the rich few and the vast urban underclass remained vividly present in all accounts of the city.

Almost exactly a hundred years after Melville's horrifying encounter, in 1930, Bessie Braddock, a young city councillor later to find fame as a battling Liverpool MP, stood for election as the Labour candidate in St Anne's ward, which contained within it the Brownlow Hill workhouse – later demolished to become the site of the new Catholic cathedral. On one of her rounds of her constituents she was invited into a room: 'In one corner was a coffin containing the corpse of an old woman. In another corner her daughter had just given birth. In the corridor behind me were three more children who had been locked out of their 'home' while the confinement took place. I can see that room now, and I will never forget the horror of it.' Poverty and appalling housing conditions of a very primitive kind persisted in Liverpool well into the twentieth century, when children of poor families still ran around the cobbled streets in bare feet. My father was one of them.

Small wonder that a kind of folk memory of poverty and hard times affects so many people in the city, informing their jokes, their attitude to those set above them in the social hierarchy, their sense of the fragility of the deal life offers.

And in the 1840s the ranks of Liverpool's poor were swelled by an even more desperate influx of people from Ireland when the potato crop failed and emigration, which had always been a choice for the rural Irish poor, became a torrent. Liverpool was, for some, a stage in the journey to America, but thousands got no further than Liverpool. Even before the famine exodus, the Irish – and again and again they are described in this way as a vast undifferentiated mass: 'the Irish' – were used to seasonal migrations looking for work in the fields. Melville encountered a group of these Irish agricultural labourers who had come over on cattle boats for the harvest:

> One morning, going into the town, I heard a tramp, as of a drove of buffaloes, behind me; and turning round, beheld the entire middle of the street filled by a great crowd of these men, who had just emerged from Brunswick Dock gates, arrayed in long-tailed coats of hoddin-gray, corduroy knee-breeches, and shod with shoes that raised a mighty dust. Flourishing their Donnybrook shillelahs, they looked like an irruption of barbarians. They were marching straight out of town into the country; and perhaps out of consider-ation for the finances of the corporation, took the middle of the street, to save the side-walks.

Singing, laughing, tossing their sticks in the air, the 'barbar-ians' without doubt were enjoying themselves.

On Melville's ship on the return journey to New York the cabin passengers would be roped off from the emigrant section 'to protect this detachment of gentility from the barbarian incursions of the "*wild Irish*" emigrants'. This was just before the desperate wave of famine emigration which would bring a grimmer human cargo unlikely to have been doing much singing and dancing. For them Liverpool was, in the words of John Denvir, in *The Life Story of an Old Rebel* (1910), 'the main artery through which the flying people poured to escape from what seemed a doomed land. Many thousands could get no further, and the condition of the already overcrowded parts of the town in which our people lived became terrible: for the wretched people brought with them the dreaded Famine Fever, and Liverpool became a plague-stricken city'. Most of the Irish immigrants poured through the Clarence Dock and the first object they would see over the Clarence Dock wall was an effigy of St Patrick, with a shamrock in his hand as if welcoming them from Ireland, placed high on the wall of a public house kept by a retired Irish pugilist, Jack Langan. They had local organisations like the Ancient Order of Hibernians, made up of Irish Liverpudlians or those of Irish descent, pledged to offer hospitality and help to their compatriots and, as Denvir puts it, to 'protect their emigrant sisters from all harm and temptation, so that they should still be known for their chastity all over the world'. There was an uneasy relationship between some of these organisations with their secret passwords and ribbons and the Catholic hierarchy who opposed secret societies, but many of the dock labourers were 'Irish ribbon-men'. Liverpool-based Fenians such as John Ryan, the most active organiser in the city, continued to work for the cause. Ryan helped to arrange the escape of the Fenian leader James Stephens from prison in Dublin in a fishing boat owned by Pat De Lacy Garton, an Irish fish merchant in Liverpool who was a councillor for Scotland ward. Later, on 29th November 1879, 50,000 Liverpool Irishmen attended a meeting at St George's Hall to hear Parnell speak. And from 1885 the Scotland Division MP was a prominent Irish Nationalist, T. P. O'Connor.

The Scotland Road area just north of the city centre was the most densely populated Irish district in what was the most densely populated British city in the nineteenth century. In 1841 the average density in England and Wales was 275 persons per square mile. In Liverpool it was 138,224. In a famous report to Parliament in 1844 by the Public Health Officer for Liverpool, Dr William H. Duncan, it was claimed that between Great Crosshall Street and Addison Street in the north end of Liverpool, a population of 7938 occupied 811 houses covering an area of 4900 square feet, which gave it a ratio of 657,963 persons per square mile. This was double the most recent figures for the most crowded parts of London. 52 of every 200 Liverpool children died before their fifth birthday. In 1841 the Irish-born population of Vauxhall, St Paul's, Exchange, and Scotland wards totalled nearly 25,000.

By 1851, following the famine, the number had increased to nearly 42,000, more than lived in most Irish towns. In these parts of Liverpool the Irish formed about half the population. De Tocqueville claimed in 1835 that there were already 60,000 Irish Catholics in the city.

One of that nameless mass of poor Irish in Vauxhall, living in a cellar in Stockdale Street, was my great-great-great-grandfather, James Murray, a shoemaker from County Mayo. Tough as the living conditions were, the alternative at home must have been worse.

Many of the Irish arrivals were sick and starving and many did not survive long. As the *Liverpool Mercury* for 15 January 1847 observed, 'The numbers of starving Irish men, women and children daily landed on our quays is appalling; and the parish of Liverpool has at present the painful and most costly task of keeping them alive, if possible.' It was indeed an impossible task and there were countless horrifying reports of the sufferings of the Irish immigrants, such as eight-year-old Luke Brothers, whose family received three shillings a week from the parish (one shilling of which was retained by the neighbour who collected it). Luke died on 8th May 1847. The post-mortem report stated there was not 'the least particle of food in the stomach'. On the mud floor of the room in Banastre Street in which Luke died there were five people. All of them were suffering from typhus. Another Irish woman, Sarah Burns, died on 23rd December 1846, after complaining of pains in the head and chest. At the inquest it was revealed that the mother of seven had eaten only one piece of bread between Sunday and her death on the Tuesday. The coroner and his jury visited the wretched mud-floored cellar where the family lived and reported: 'A person could not stand up in it, the floor was composed of mud; and in that hovel there were seventeen human beings crowded together without even so much as a bit of straw to lie down on. We felt convinced that if they were allowed to remain in their present condition there would be two or three deaths before many days'. Sarah Burns and her seven children had been on the streets begging in order to survive and the verdict on the mother was that she had '[died] from disease of the lungs accelerated by the want of the common necessities of life'. The French visitor Hippolyte Taine was probably not exaggerating when he said of the Liverpool Irish in the 1860s: 'their quarter is the lowest circle of hell'.

Not all Liverpool's Irish population, however, was Catholic. Clashes between Protestant and Catholic mobs are a well-attested Liverpool tradition, though now they have disappeared. In the Orange processions to commemorate the Battle of the Boyne on 12th July, the largest contingent was the ship's carpenters. Some even called it 'Carpenters' Day'. No Catholic could get work as a ship's carpenter and it was only the rise of iron ships that broke up that particular monopoly. I recall a big, tough boy at school called Ruane who sang snatches of a provocative song used to taunt the other side on 'Orangemen's Day' as we called it. It went something like: 'My Uncle Mick/Took a great big stick/And he went off to the slaughter;/He killed ten thousand Orangemen/At the Battle of Boyne Water'.

Other kinds of disorder were prevalent in the dockside areas of Liverpool. As early as 1808 the anonymous author of *Liverpool, a Satire* inveighed against the influx of bad elements into the city from all around:

> Now range the docks, perambulate the quay
> And all the western boundary survey –
> Tumultous uproars waken all your fears,
> And blasphemy provokes your startled ears.

The best we can say about this poem is that it is 'School of Roscoe', but it highlights a feature of Liverpool's reputation in the first half of the nineteenth century that earned it the name 'the Black Spot on the Mersey'. In the first three decades of the century the population doubled and the old municipal organisation of law and order couldn't cope with the surging population. According to W. R. Cockcroft, historian of Liverpool's police force in the nineteenth century, '[quayside] violence in particular gave Liverpool an evil reputation, and the frequent cases of stabbings were encouraged by the common practice among sailors until the 1860s of carrying a sheath dagger'. Sailors were generally turned loose from their ships while they lay in dock and the combination of drink, time on their hands, and weapons had inevitable results in and around the waterfront and the city's 'singing saloons' such as the Sans Pareil, the Liver, the Queen's Theatre, the Custom House, or the Penny Hop. Drunkenness, prostitution, thieving, and juvenile delinquency were rife. Thousands of abandoned, neglected or homeless children without education or occupation roamed the streets or hung around outside these low theatres. In the 1830s in the Borough of Liverpool it was estimated that there were 1200 public houses, taps, gin palaces, and penny ale cellars. Attempts were made to counter this with temperance societies such as the David Jones Society, established in Scotland Road in 1835, but trade continued to flourish. A report to the Constabulary Committee in 1837 estimated that there were 520 brothels in Liverpool with an average of four prostitutes in each, together with 625 'houses of ill fame' and 136 common lodging houses also used for prostitution. Liverpool had become one of the most notorious centres for prostitution outside London, with young girls of Irish parentage, according to the report, being commonplace. The rough neighbourhoods frequented by sailors were, Melville found, 'putrid with vice and crime; to which, perhaps, the round globe does not furnish a parallel. The sooty and begrimed bricks of the very houses have a reeking, Sodom-like, and murderous look... These are the haunts from which sailors sometimes disappear forever; or issue in the morning, robbed naked, from the broken doorways'.

One group of sailors, however, who held their heads high in Liverpool, to the slightly unsettled apprehension of Melville, were the black seamen. He noted:

> In Liverpool indeed the negro steps with a prouder pace, and lifts his head like a man; for here, no such exaggerated feeling exists in respect to him, as in America. Three or four times, I encountered our black steward, dressed very handsomely, and walking arm in arm with a good-looking English woman. In New York, such a couple would have been mobbed in three minutes; and the steward would have been lucky to escape with whole limbs. Owing to the friendly reception extended to them, and the unwonted immunities they enjoy in Liverpool, the black cooks and stewards of American ships are very much attached to the place and like to make voyages to it.

On 19th July 1839 an advertisement was placed in the *Liverpool Mercury* announcing that the *St Lawrence* was to sail on 1st August for New York. The vessel was described as 'a very desirable conveyance for goods and passengers' and the latter were advised to address themselves to Captain Brown, on board, at Prince's Dock. On the day of sailing, after four days of contrary winds, 'a vast fleet of merchantmen, all steering broad out to sea' finally left the port. 'The white sails glistened in the clear morning air like a great Eastern encampment of sultans', and Melville, together with those roped-off, huddled masses of slightly luckier Irish emigrants, was heading back to New York.

9

Court Life

On 13th May 1854 my great-grandfather, William Murray, was born at 12 Court, Thomas Street, Liverpool. For someone who worked – like Felix Spencer, the model for Gerald Manley Hopkins' Felix Randal – in a 'random, grim forge' it sounds a rather elegant address, borrowing something from the regal associations of the word 'court'. But William, and Mary his wife (the daughter of a house-painter called Doherty from County Wexford), lived in one of the most notorious kinds of dwelling in nineteenth-century Liverpool.

The courts were clusters of dwellings reached by a narrow tunnel that would appear in a terraced street of houses and along which one would pass into a dark, dank space flanked on either side by dwellings, running at right angles to the houses fronting the street, with the sole sanitary facilities for all out in the common yard. Here is Pat O'Mara's description of 14 Court, Stanhope Street, in *The Autobiography of a Liverpool Slummy*:

> The term, of course, is ironic; what the 'Court' represented
> was a narrow alley receding off the street to a larger areaway,

like an unseen tooth cavity, and ending in a conglomeration of filthy shacks. About twenty-five large families – dock labourers, hawkers, sooty artisans and their children – lived in the average court. Two revoltingly dirty toilets stood in the areaway and were always in demand; a queue usually waited in line, newspapers in hand. The shacks were so closely packed together and their walled partitions so thin that one had no choice but to listen to what went on on either side. Screams often rent the air at night, one court waylaying another in the darkness. The cheaper elderly whores favoured the courts, and could always be found attending to their furtive business in the darker corners. Huge cats continually stalked the place, their eyes an eerie phosphorescence in the darkness.

Dr William Duncan's 1844 public health report, already referred to, found that 64 per cent of people in the Exchange ward (this contained Launcelott's Hey through which Melville passed and where he watched the woman and her children die of starvation) lived in either courts or cellars. These dwellings should have been swept away by the twentieth century but the Second World War delayed slum clearance and as late as 1951 there were examples still standing. Former sanitary inspector Brian Ahier Read in his *Vanished Liverpool and the San'tree Man* (2001) describes the surviving courts he found in the Scotland Road area in 1951:

> The 'court' was a central yard about four metres wide and ten metres long. On each side of this yard were three-storey houses with one small room on each floor. There was no window at the back because that was the wall of the house belonging to the adjoining court. The only amenities for court houses were a stand pipe for water in the centre of the court and two primitive trough closets at the ends of the courts. (A trough closet is simply a long channel with seats built over it. The wastes are washed down a drain whenever

one of the users takes the trouble to fetch a bucket of water for this purpose.)

William and Mary could at least reflect that for them, unlike their grandfather, James Murray, who lived in the one thing worse than a court, an earth-floored cellar, things were improving. Halfway through the nineteenth century, the Murrays had reached ground level.

Social reformers – as often as not in clerical garb – have provided copious descriptions of these dark 'hell-holes', as Bessie Braddock would later describe their successors in her maiden speech to Parliament in 1945. The Reverend Hugh Stowell Brown in one of his *Twelve Lectures to the Men of Liverpool* (1858) made the familiar contrast, in his eighth lecture, 'The Street', between the naming of the most poverty-stricken streets in Liverpool after the poets (Great Homer Street – site of 'Paddy's Market' – Virgil Street, Dryden Street) and the grim reality: 'these delightful retreats of the muses and masses [are] illumined with the glare of a hundred gin shops, redolent with the fumes of tobacco and whiskey, reeking with indescribable filth, and swarming with men, women, and children, for the most part dirty, ragged and wretched'. Many of the streets lived in by the poor, he noted, were

> insufferably nasty; the houses, built in that style called jerry building, for which Liverpool is rather celebrated, are ready to tumble down. There is no sewerage, or if there be it is not worthy of the name, for the stagnant water poisons the whole street; the decencies of civilised life can scarcely be observed. Fever, small-pox, and consumption have taken up their abode in those wretched regions, and there they will remain, glutting themselves on the miserable inhabitants.

The courts, in particular, were built 'in such close proximity as to expel both light and air' and they were 'for men abodes that are not fit for beasts... there is no drainage whatever... the filth is unbearable and the stench enough to poison a dog... There are faces to be seen that do not appear to have been washed these twenty years, and there are floors and furniture that have never been swept or dusted at all'. In his *Autobiography* (1887), Brown referred to the cellars, which were if anything even worse than the courts, as 'no better than preparatory graves (they cannot even be called, in the language of the Necropolis "tidy graves")'.

Men such as Hugh Stowell Brown were convinced of one thing: nothing would change until the swinish proles changed their habits: 'The people have the remedy for this state of things in their own hands; no one can help them if they do not help themselves; they can move out of those back slums if they will.' The surprise is that more did not do so, if all it took was a little will-power.

Political change, especially socialist change, was out of the question for these clerics and even Pat O'Mara's unsparing early-twentieth-century account is strangely bereft of the slightest political understanding of his people's predicament: facing acute and desperate poverty in one of the most prosperous ports of the Empire. In Brown's view, set out in another lecture, 'Cleanliness is Next to Godliness', there were two major obstacles to the poor walking away from their degradation: 'Drink and dirt are the devil's foremen; he pays them liberally; their wages are thousands of bodies and souls'. The standpipe was in place, as we have seen, to deal with the dirt so all that remained was to renounce the demon drink. In the accounts given by the Christian temperance movement the baroque gin palaces – and even today Liverpool has some magnificent boozers, such as the *art nouveau* Philharmonic Hotel ('the Phil') or the Crown near Lime Street Station – are described with a lip-smacking prurient relish:

The greatest pains are taken to render these places attractive; they are fitted up regardless of expense, but it pays to make them splendid; so they are, for the most part, well-situated at the corners of the streets; the windows are of superb plate-glass; the gas fittings very ornamental; and outside, over the door, there is invariably a great lamp. Sometimes this lamp is very appropriately made in the shape of a barrel, with staves of red and white glass alternated. Occasionally the lamp has a revolving light, being thereby all the more likely to attract attention.

Sounds a great place for a bevvy.

Half a century later, James Samuelson, in *The Children of Our Slums* (1911), found a similar picture: 'Leaving the commercial centre of prosperous Liverpool [at this time Liverpool had probably reached the peak of its success as a port] and descending from the tramcar after a ride of a few minutes, we traverse streets of which the squalor is not redeemed by their having been honoured with the names of some of the world's greatest poets such as Homer and Virgil'. Samuelson had reached Scotland Road. He too described the courts and the cellars – and, once again it is worth remembering that these were still inhabited in places at the beginning of the twentieth century:

On entering the cellar one is repelled by the foul atmosphere, nor is this to be wondered at when the contents are considered. The cellar is about ten feet by fourteen in dimensions and is lighted by a small window looking on to the area. Against this stands a sewing machine, with some unfinished work; in this instance a coarse, holland apron. Besides this, there is a couple of chairs and against the wall on the far side of the hearth is a dilapidated bedstead with poor, disarranged coverings. The foot of the bed touches the table, so that there is hardly room to pass between them.

A few tiny pictures, in discoloured frames, and a crucifix, serve as ornaments over the mantlepiece. A small recess in the wall appears to be used as a dressing-room, and on the far side of the cellar is a doorway leading to the yard. In this single apartment there lives (if it can be called living) a family of five.

In 1908, the year of the introduction of the Children Act, 1209 cellars in Liverpool were legally occupied. Samuelson recalled another, much earlier memory, from the visit by the British Association to Liverpool in 1870. He went on an inspection of the slums with Thomas Henry Huxley and others and saw 'nine dock porters, fully-clothed, sleeping in three beds, in one room, in a lodging house'. If Godliness depended on cleanliness it is small wonder that the clergymen were so glum.

The condition of the Liverpool poor in the nineteenth century is well documented. In 1842 John Finch published his pioneering social survey, *Statistics of Vauxhall Ward, Liverpool*, written 'with the view of shewing the actual condition of the labouring classes, and giving it the publicity it appeared to require'. Partly sponsored by the Liverpool Anti-Monopoly Association, it was striking a blow for free trade at the same time as highlighting the sufferings of 'the labouring population'. The report came with various letters appended from bakers and other tradesmen testifying to the detrimental effect on their businesses of poverty and of the wickedness of monopoly. Street by street (as many as 25 courts opened off some streets) the demographic facts for the ward's population of 5000 were accumulated. The report found that large numbers of the Liverpool working class were actually 'natives of agricultural districts, and that the number of them is annually increasing... by this migration, the landed interest... avoid the maintenance of their own poor'. Some of the poor in the courts and cellars managed, unbelievably, to sub-let unofficially – which make the figures for population density and overcrowding certainly underestimates.

Overall, the survey showed how naïve the preachers and spouters at the audiences of working men were in thinking that mass urban poverty could simply be shrugged off. 'I found one poor woman,' reported one of the team of researchers, John Holme, 'with three or four children (one of them sucking at the breast) who had not tasted food for two days. The husband said, they had a good house and furniture before work became so slack, but they had been obliged to sell all; the last articles were four chairs, which they sold for eight shillings.'

Another recorder of the facts of mid-nineteenth-century working-class life was the journalist Hugh Shimmin, one of those almost-forgotten Liverpool figures – a sort of Liverpool Mayhew – whose writing ought to be better known. A rough diamond, Shimmin was born in Whitehaven in Cumbria, of Manx stock, coming to Liverpool as a child when his father got work on the docks as a repair and maintenance worker. Shimmin himself was apprenticed to a bookbinder and he soon threw himself into the work of self-improvement. Like many reforming observers he was anti-drink and was a member of James Martineau's Paradise Street Unitarian Chapel. He joined the Mechanics' Institute and the Mental Improvement Society and taught in the latter's pioneering 'ragged schools'. He was deliberately unpretentious in his dress, rather unkempt and contemptuous of middle-class norms. Eventually he bought the bookbinding business and became owner and editor of a journal called the *Porcupine* (a suitably prickly title for his costive talents), in which most of his journalism appeared.

In 1855–56 Shimmin wrote a series of articles in the *Liverpool Mercury* which became a book, *Liverpool Life: Its Pleasures, Practices and Pastimes*, whose title page banner 'Publicity the true cure of social evils' was there to insure him against the charge that his subject matter was merely scandalous and sensational. In fact there was a good market, especially from the godly, for lurid descriptions of low-life and vice. In 1857 he wrote a series of satirical portraits of Liverpool town councillors in the *Mercury* which came out as a book in 1866, *Pen and Ink Sketches of Liverpool Town Councillors*. In 1860 he became editor of *Porcupine*. Essentially a Liberal, Shimmin campaigned in his journalism on housing and sanitary issues and his exposure of conditions in the back streets and courts, in the view of his modern editors, John Walton and Alastair Wilcox (who have brought together a very valuable selection of his writing, *Low Life and Improvement in Mid-Victorian England* (1991)), 'made a major contribution to the Liverpool Sanitary Amendment Act 1864' – which sounds, from what we have noted above, like a very needful contribution. When he went so far as to accuse the local shipping magnates of having been involved in insurance scams (in a piece called 'Ocean Thuggism') he was jailed for libel.

Shimmin's colourful journalism is stronger on description than analysis (a feature of Victorian social reportage on Liverpool) but it does take us on a journey into the life of the urban poor of the city. A piece called 'An hour in a grog shop', for example, paints a Saturday night scene of a woman going in search of her hard-drinking husband, 'the wife lean and vixenish, the children pallid and ragged'. She tracks him down to a gin palace where he is engaged in the sport of 'tossing' for who will buy the next round of quart pots of ale. Inside this lurid drinking-den we see 'girls, boys, women, old men, robust villains, slender mechanics, oyster men, stay-lace women, dog fanciers, street musicians, a comic vocalist'. In another excursion, Shimmin visits 'The Free and Easy', a place of 'ballad singing and beer drinking'. The Free and Easy was a sort of working-class mutual society aimed at raising money, rather like a Christmas club, for special celebrations. In this visit in November 1857, Shimmin passed in the street outside people selling 'watercress, pigs' feet, coloured sweets, stay laces, boys' caps and pickled cockles', and ascended to an upper room containing 84 working men where a young man was singing (very badly) 'The Lass of Richmond Hill'. The song ended with ribald calls for the singer to 'put his head in a rat hole for half an hour'.

There were also certain Free and Easys frequented by toffs in areas where the so-called 'milliner's shops' or brothels did good business – with women looking out for 'queer fish on the loose' who could be fleeced. Shimmin reported on 'The Free Concert Room' in Williamson Square late on a Saturday night. The upstairs 'concert room' in this instance held 38 people including 'carters, bakers, shoemakers and sailors' – the foreign tars in the company of various 'disorderly and drunken women'. A crummy-sounding show was put on of 'Adam and Eve in Paradise' with women in flesh-tights performing bad songs and executing clog dances. Shimmin moved off to another concert room where there were more obscene songs and step-dancing with over-priced (and sometimes adulterated) drink together with amateur performers. Shimmin, who like most people blamed the demon drink for all these social evils, exclaimed for the benefit of his readers: 'What a preparation for the Sabbath!'

Shimmin's Liverpool in mid-century was Britain's second city. Its population in 1861 was 444,000 and commercial and port-related activitites provided most of the jobs – which were nonethless very insecure because based on a system of casual labour. As Walton and Wilcox put it: 'For the majority of working class Liverpudlians life was of necessity a hand-to-mouth existence, with no real chance of saving or insuring against contingencies. The poverty of central Liverpool was endemic and notorious.' Most women worked in poorly paid jobs such as domestic service and dressmaking, and padded out household income by chopping and selling kindling, taking in washing, keeping small shops in front rooms and cellars, and lending money at punitive rates of interest to people who were slightly worse off than themselves. Even the washing taken in could be pawned to cover cash flow in the middle of the week. Pat O'Mara describes the activities of the 'Fish and Money women' of a slightly later period, but they would have been established in Shimmin's day:

> The technique went something like this: they would come up our entry with baskets of putrid fish and inquire who among the men had 'got on' down at the dock [a reference to the casual hiring of dock labour day to day in Liverpool]. Thus if any of the men's wives were courageous enough to borrow four shillings in cash, they would also have to take two shillings' worth of this putrid fish. The debt would therefore stand at six shillings to be paid on the following Saturday – or else. My father was always in debt to the fish-and-money people but was also very discreet in paying them their debts. The fish he would throw into the darkness of the entry, there to add to the general stink of the place and to be set upon by huge mangy cats.

O'Mara told of an old woman, Mrs Haggerty, who would regularly pawn her false teeth every Monday morning. When she died the pawnbroker 'hopefully put them up for sale in his front window'. There were no takers and eventually they were banished to his store room.

But the only remedy for this urban wretchedness continued to be general moral exhortation rather than any kind of social rearrangement. Hugh Stowell Brown again, thundering to 'the working men of Liverpool' at one of his popular lectures at the Concert Hall, which sometimes attracted audiences of 2000 people, drew the following conclusion:

> Contentment is a lesson often inculcated upon the poor, but I wish that in one sense they were discontented; I wish that they felt an unspeakable repugnance to the filthy habitations in which they are huddled together. I would say – Don't be discontented with the Constitution, for there is no better under the sun; don't be discontented with work, for work is the wise and benevolent ordinance of God; don't think of agitating for the Charter, for Socialism, Communism, and all that nonsense; but be discontented with dirt, and darkness, and foul air, and bad smells, and undrained streets, and jerry-built houses, and set to work resolutely to free yourselves from this wretchedness.

The reaction of 'the working men of Liverpool', at whom these lectures were aimed, to Hugh Stowell Brown's effrontery is not recorded.

The wretchedness deepened. Over the decade 1861–1870 the average death rate in England was 22 per 1000 people. In Liverpool it was 33 but in the oldest part of central Liverpool, the parish of Liverpool, it rose to 40. In that same parish infant mortality was over 300 per 1000 with the under-fives accounting for half of all deaths. There were, of course, variations between the rich and poor areas. In 1871 the death rate in Vauxhall ward was 43 per 1000 but in elegant Rodney Street it was only 23.4. Of these deaths, 40 per cent were from infectious diseases linked to environmental conditions. When the 1864 Liverpool Sanitary Amendment Act was brought in the domestic inspectors reported on overcrowded living conditions which forced adult daughters to share beds with their parents, and adult brothers and sisters to share the same bed.

I remember a snatch of a humorous song being sung by one of my uncles that began 'There were five in the bed by the old Pier Head'. Clearly, this would have been a modest level of occupancy in the mid-Victorian period.

Charles Dickens also ventured into the sleazy parts of Liverpool at the same time as Shimmin, reporting his findings in *The Uncommercial Traveller* (1860). Dickens set out as a temporary member of the Liverpool police force to see for himself how sailors in the port were regularly fleeced by the locals, a habit that persisted into the early twentieth century, according to Pat O'Mara, who describes some techniques of 'sailor-baiting' – luring sailors into houses (often with some slyly hinted sexual bait) in order to relieve them of their money. Dickens calls his typical visiting tar Mercantile Jack – one of those 'ill-lodged, ill-fed, ill-used, hocussed, entrapped, anticipated, cleaned out' seamen who wandered the streets between voyages. 'As I walked the dock-quays at Liverpool,' Dickens reported, 'there Mercantile Jack was, and very busy he was, and very cold he was: the snow yet lying in the frozen furrows of the land, and the north-east winds snipping off the tops of the little waves in the Mersey, and rolling them into hailstones to pelt him with.'

Dickens has a description of a 'singing-house' which is exactly like Shimmin's upper concert rooms: 'About the room some amazing coffee-coloured pictures varnished an inch deep, and some stuffed creatures in cases...' Here foreign sailors watched 'the young lady dancing the hornpipe'. Dickens moved on to another pub where black sailors congregated. Seeming to contradict Melville's claim that black sailors met no prejudice in Liverpool, Dickens observed: 'They generally kept together, these poor fellows, said Mr Superintendent, because they were at a disadvantage singly, and liable to slights in the neighbouring streets'. Together with the constables of the

watch, Dickens prowled the rough streets back from the waterfront into the small hours:

> for miles and hours we explored a strange world, where
> nobody ever goes to bed, but everybody is sitting up,
> waiting for Jack. This exploration was among a labyrinth
> of dismal courts and blind alleys, called Entries, kept in
> wonderful order by the police, and in much better order
> than by the corporation: the want of gaslight in the most
> dangerous and infamous places being quite unworthy of
> so spirited a town.

Some of these houses where reception committees awaited
the unwary sailor were reached by 'noisome passages so
profoundly dark that we felt our way with our hands' and one
consisted of 'a nauseous room with an earth floor, into which
the refuse scum of an alley trickled. The stench of this habi-
tation was abominable; the seeming poverty of it, diseased
and dire... Three weird old women of transcendent ghastli-
ness, were at needlework at a table in this room.' They were
stitching money bags.

'Evermore,' reflected Dickens later, 'when on a breezy day
I see poor Mercantile Jack running into port with a fair wind
under sail, I shall think of the unsleeping host of devourers
who never go to bed, and are always in their set traps waiting
for him.'

More powerful, however, than anything reported by
Dickens, was that extraordinary imaginative by-product of
nineteenth-century Liverpool: Heathcliff. In Emily Brontë's
Wuthering Heights, Mr Earnshaw returns from a visit to the
city clutching a 'dirty, ragged, black-haired child' speaking an
incomprehensible gibberish. This mixed-race child, possibly
the product of a liaison between a Liverpool woman and a
foreign sailor, was found 'starving, and houseless, and as good

as dumb, in the streets of Liverpool; where he picked it up and inquired for its owner'. There is only one Heathcliff in English fiction but the starving, the dirty and the ragged in Victorian Liverpool ran into tens of thousands.

10

The Sea Bathing Lake

Some years ago, when I was trying to make a living as a freelance journalist, I arrived one blustery, bright autumn morning in Southport, the once genteel seaside resort north of Liverpool, to interview some local government planning officials. The trade magazine which had recently commissioned me to write an article about municipal rubbish collection in Wigan (that town, it seemed, was at the cutting edge of the muck business in the 1990s) now wanted a piece on – what? I have long forgotten. Since I was living in Wales, the London editors assumed that the north of England could also be considered part of my patch. After an hour or so with my planners I was free to wander through the town, across the cast iron bridges over the boating ponds, in the direction of the sea. What I saw – or more correctly, what I did not see – brought me to an abrupt and astonished halt.

Like someone patting his inside pockets to discover with horror that his wallet has been stolen by a pickpocket, I gazed at a large expanse of green turf in disbelief. Where had it gone? On this very spot, throughout my childhood, and, I assumed, for all time, had stood my summer Shangri-La or Land of Cockayne, the Sea Bathing Lake. Gone were the green cast iron turnstiles at the ticket office, the loud din of hundreds of Liverpudlians around the large open-air pool, the bronzed, preening life-guards, the smooth metal water slides, the row upon row of canvas club-chairs, the changing rooms where men whistled loudly since there were no locks on the half-doors, the Brylcreem machine where, for an old penny, one could get a squirt of white goo to smear on one's hair before leaving, the grey metal clothes horses one dressed with one's clothes before handing them over to bald attendants in exchange for a metal disk on a rubber ankle-ring, the shallow pools of white disinfectant through which one waded on the way to the pool, the salty taste of the briny water, the floating platforms one could swim out to, the overall sense of gaiety and noise and splashing enthusiasm. Vanished!

Summer days at the Sea Bathing Lake were punctuated by family picnics around the pool, which consisted of tomato sandwiches, banana sandwiches and – the mere thought of it – jam sandwiches. Jam sarnies! I can still hear the clatter of feet on the planks of the wooden bridges over the Marine Lake as we strode towards the pool. There is a photograph in a family album which shows my parents, newly married, not long after the war, marching forward with their swimming costumes tightly rolled in a towel under the arm, something in their confident stride emblematic of the new world into which so many Britons were stepping in the late 1940s and 1950s, a world of semi-detached houses, washing machines, then fridges and cars, a land fit for consumers.

Southport was a favourite summer or weekend destination, near enough to bicycle to, and no time at all in the new black Ford Popular with its registration number PKA 2 (surely changing hands as I write for a considerable amount of money among specialist number plate collectors). Southport was the shops and Victorian arcades, the Kardomah Café, or, on very special occasions, afternoon tea of toasted teacakes with silver service and crisp white linen at the tea-room of Marshall and Snelgrove's department store. The sea itself, at Southport, always seemed a very long way away, across the hard, flat, windswept sands and visible only at high tide. South of the town the beaches and sand dunes stretched towards Liverpool, getting progressively more polluted and mucky as one approached the docks at Seaforth. I used to love wandering as a child in the dunes at Formby and Freshfield, reached by the electric train that ran through the flat landscape of dunes, pinewoods and golf courses and which is captured so perfectly in Beryl Bainbridge's fine novel, *Harriet Said...* (1972). That lonely, desolate, featureless landscape was the perfect backdrop for the cultivation of adolescent melancholia: I have become far too cheerful these days to be able any longer to appreciate it properly.

These high sandhills with their soft sand and spiky marram grass, windswept and with an uninspiring view of the Mersey estuary flowing out to the Irish Sea, were the scene, in November 1856, of an unusual encounter between two of the greatest nineteenth-century American writers, Nathaniel Hawthorne and Herman Melville.

Hawthorne first arrived in Liverpool on the Cunard steamer *Niagara* in July 1853 to take up the post of American consul in Liverpool, staying first at the Waterloo Hotel, then at lodgings in Duke Street run by a Mrs Blodgett and then at the Rock Ferry Hotel. His first impressions were lukewarm:

> My office consists of two rooms in an edifice called Washington Buildings, and so named from the circumstances of the consulate being located here. It is near the docks, and on the corner of Brunswick-street; and from my window, across the narrow street, I have a view of a tall, dismal, smoke-

blackened, ugly brick warehouse, – uglier than any building I ever saw in America; and from one of the various stories, bags of salt are often being raised and lowered, swinging and vibrating in the air... Since I have been in Liverpool we have hardly had a day, until yesterday, without more or less of rain, and so cold and shivery that life was miserable.

Hawthorne spent a lot of time complaining about his posting – 'brutal captains and brutish sailors... calls of idleness or ceremony from my travelling countrymen' – and considered that '[the] Mersey has the colour of a mud-puddle, and no atmospheric effect, as far as I have seen, ever gives it a more agreeable tinge'. His *English Notebooks* are filled with disagreeable observations, not least about the human element. One day in August 1853 he took a trip up and down the Mersey on a boat from Rock Ferry and was struck by the freedom and boisterousness of the Liverpool crowd on deck, a liberty of behaviour he was not used to. 'In fact, men and women here do things that would at least make them ridiculous in America. They are not afraid to enjoy themselves in their own way, and have no pseudo-gentility to support.' As a thumbnail sketch of the Scouse disposition this is hard to beat.

Yet Hawthorne's observations of Liverpool in the middle of the nineteenth century are always interesting. In November he noted: 'There is a heavy dun fog on the river, and over the city, today; the very gloomiest atmosphere that ever I was acquainted with. On the river, the steamboats strike gongs or ring bells, to give warning of their approach. There are lamps burning in the counting rooms and entries of the warehouses, and they gleam distinctly through the windows.' But as with Melville it was the poverty that struck him most forcefully:

Yetserday [3rd December 1853], a chill, misty December day, yet I saw a woman barefooted in the street, not to speak of children...

Chill, frosty weather [13th December 1853]... Yet I saw a barefooted young woman yesterday. The feet of these poor creatures have exactly the red complexion of their hands, acquired by constant exposure to the cold air.

I see nothing more disgusting than the women and girls here in Liverpool, who pick up horsedung in the streets – rushing upon the treasure, the moment it is dropt, taking it up by handsfull and putting it in their baskets. Some are old women; some marriageable girls, and not uncomely girls, were they well dressed and clean. What a business this is!

On 28th February 1856, Hawthorne paid a visit to the West Derby Workhouse which opened his eyes still further to the hardships faced by the Liverpool poor. At the end of his tour, the workhouse Governor 'showed us a shed or outhouse, inside of which were piled up an immense quantity of new coffins, of the plainest and cheapest description'. This was where the poor went to die. But it was the river that he kept on coming back to: 'and truly this river Mersey is never without a breeze, and generally in the direction of its course – an evil-tempered, unkindly, blustering wind too, like the worst temper of an Englishman – a wind that you cannot face without being exasperated by it... I have undergone very miserable hours on the Mersey.'

During his four years in Liverpool, Hawthorne did no creative writing, except for these copious notebook entries, which might have accounted for some of his sourness and frustration. Eventually, in the summer of 1856, for the sake of the health of his wife, Sophia, he moved his family from the centre of Liverpool to Southport and commuted back and forth on the railway. The move did nothing to lighten his spirits:

The ride is through a most uninteresting tract of country...
a wide monotony of level plain, and here and there a
village and a church; almost always a windmill in sight,
there being plenty of breeze to turn its sails, on this windy
coast. The railway skirts along the sea, the whole distance,
but is shut out from the sight of it by the low sandhills
which seem to have been heaped up by the waves. There
are one or two light-houses on the shore. I have not seen a
drearier landscape, even in Lancashire.

As summer gave way to autumn the winds continued to blow.

Brought up on that same 'windy coast' where the sea
breezes rattled our windows and deposited a sandy film on the
glass panes, I can appreciate Hawthorne's difficulty in coming
to terms with this 'dreary and howling blast'. He noted, on
the way to Southport, how the trees had been deformed by
the constant sea breezes: 'invariably their branches, and the
whole contour and attitude of the tree, turned from seaward,
with a strangely forlorn aspect'. At Southport itself, on 'this
bleak and blasty shore of the Irish sea', the weather ensured
that it was always 'an awfully windy place, especially here
on the Promenade [Hawthorne lived in Brunswick Terrace];
always a whistle and a howl – always an eddying gust through
the passages and chambers – often a patter of rain, or hail
or snow, against the windows; and, in the long evenings, the
sounds are very much as if it were on shipboard in mid-ocean,
with the waves dashing against the vessel's sides'.

Like countless generations of Lancashire and Liverpudlian
holidaymakers at Southport, Hawthorne noticed the strange
absence and withdrawal of the sea itself. All he seemed to see
was the 'bare, pool-strewn waste of sands'. He noted that 'in
all my experience of Southport, I have not yet seen the sea, but
only an interminable breadth of sands, stretching out to the
horizon... but no expanse of water... low water and intermi-

nable sands'. Only once, on a late February morning in 1857, did he catch a rare glimpse of the Welsh mountains in the distance: 'How misty is England!' On the wide flat sands there were bathing machines, donkey carts that would take you out to the water's edge, and the famous 'Flying Dutchman', a sort of boat on wheels, schooner-rigged with sails, which sometimes made good speed on the sands if the wind was right. 'Southport,' moaned Hawthorne, 'is as stupid a place as ever I lived in; and I cannot but bewail an ill fortune, to have been compelled to spend these many months on these barren sands, when almost every other square yard of England contains something that would have been historically or poetically interesting. Our life here has been a blank.' Even the surrounding Lancashire countryside did nothing for him: 'it is nothing but sand-hillocks, covered with coarse grass'. He did visit Ormskirk market and bought some of its famous gingerbread which as children in the 1950s we always enjoyed as a treat on visits to the market. I hope they are making it still.

In July 1857, Hawthorne finally left Southport for good. He had received only one visitor of real interest during this period: Herman Melville, who was back in Liverpool nearly two decades after his first voyage to the port as a cabin boy. In November 1856 the two men walked out from Brunswick Terrace into those windswept Southport sandhills and sat and talked on a blustery autumn day with a gleefully shared gloom about Providence and futurity. Melville, Hawthorne noted appreciatively, had 'pretty much made up his mind to be annihilated'.

A refreshing antidote to the lowering tone of these moody New England sages, buffeted by the winds from the Irish Sea on their grassy Southport sandhill, and encumbered by awful metaphysics, is the bracing optimism of Thomas Baines, who was writing his *Liverpool in 1859* at around the same time.

Baines was a glorifier and celebrant of the great age of Victorian mercantile Liverpool. The docks, he announced in his opening pages, are 'at once the seat and the instruments of a commerce extending to every country on the face of the globe, and involving transactions amounting to upwards of one hundred millions sterling, in yearly value'. He added: 'The commerce of Liverpool is universal in its nature and vast in its extent'. Everything in Baines' account is a triumph, from the explosion of public buildings, to the size of the docks (35 feet deep, their inner walls 17 miles long, their thickness 10 feet, their average height 40 feet), to the numbers of passengers (25,000 emigrants sailed to Australia on 100 ships in 1858). In Baines' account there are no courts and cellars, poverty or disease: 'The outer part of the district of Toxteth, once a royal deer park, consists of pleasant dingles winding down to the Mersey, of natural terraces on the banks of the river, and of woody hills, nearly all of which have been converted into parks and pleasure grounds, and covered with villas and ornamental cottages'. And above all there is the bustling maritime scene:

> The vessels engaged in the steam trade of Liverpool, include every steamer now afloat, from the light ferry steamers, which dart across the Mersey in a few minutes, to the finest ocean steamer, which steams across the Atlantic, in defiance of winds and storms, maintaining the communication between the old world and the new, with a swiftness, safety and regularity, which have excited the admiration and applause of all nations.

Baines was certainly right about the splendid public buildings. The most striking of these was St George's Hall, which sits with its surrounding buildings on the plateau that is one of the first sights met by the visitor emerging from the main

Lime Street Station today. Even those of us whose taste is not for the neo-classical have to admire the construction of St George's Hall, its perfect proportion, its elegance, its confident possession of its site. If we must have neo-classical buildings then let them be as good as this. Despite having known it all my life, like many Liverpudlians I had never set foot in this building until recently, when it was restored and opened to the public as an attraction. Throughout my childhood it was blackened with soot, like all Liverpool's city centre buildings, and we were unable to see its golden stone. During its recent restoration, large signs indicated that the refurbishment was being funded by the National Lottery's Heritage Fund and by the European Union. 'We couldn't have done it without eu' said the placard nailed to the builder's security fence. I learn now that it is to be a centrepiece of the celebrations of the Capital of Culture and, what many consider to be more significant, the 2007 celebrations of the eight hundredth anniversary of the granting of a charter to Liverpool by King John in 1007.

The architect of St George's Hall was a 25-year-old Londoner, Harvey Lonsdale Elmes, who won an architectural competition to secure the commission. Work began in 1841 and the building opened in 1854. The Hall, which draws on Roman as well as Greek themes, is distinguished by its Corinthian columns and porticoes. Joseph Sharples, author of the latest Pevsner guide to Liverpool, says of the south portico: 'Towering above St John's Lane, it recalls visionary nineteenth century reconstructions of the temples in the Roman Forum'. Together with the Walker Art Gallery and the Picton Library, the Hall commands this elevated site in the city centre and symbolises the Victorian inheritance of Liverpool.

In his excellent 1967 book on art and architecture in Liverpool, *Art in a City*, John Willett observes that '[today] the nineteenth century still lies all around the artist: in the façade of the Walker Art Gallery for instance, with Raphael and Michelangelo forbiddingly enthroned either side of the portico and the substantial figure of Commerce on top'. Willett sees St George's Hall as the culmination of a movement in Liverpool's civic culture that began in the first decades of the nineteenth century with the foundation of the Liverpool Mechanics' Institution. This was started as the Liverpool Mechanics' School of Arts in 1825, with some opposition from members of the Corporation who feared that '[if] you go on in instructing the working classes, they will be so much enlightened that they will be treading on the heels of their superiors'. Artistic patronage, civic projects, enlightened politics, and the boom in the port led to something like a renaissance. As Willett puts it: 'This whole association of flourishing commerce, radical politics and the neo-classical style in art determined the artistic and intellectual climate of Liverpool in the first half of the century, and it was splendidly commemorated in the building of St George's Hall in the middle of the city... Since the building of St Paul's no British city has had such an expressive and grandly conceived central feature.'

Another magnificent architectural achievement was the construction between 1843 and 1847 of the Albert Dock. 'For sheer punch there is little in the early commercial architecture of Europe to emulate it', wrote Nikolaus Pevsner. The architect was a dour Yorkshireman from Pontefract, Jesse Hartley, who also built many of the other docks. Joseph Sharples observes: 'What solicits admiration now, apart of course from the scale, is the monumental solemnity of the warehouses, the manner in which they have been pared down to a synthesis of austere classicism and technological functionalism'. My favourite feature is the colonnade around the dock. It consists of hollow cast-iron columns, now painted red, fifteen feet high and filled with masonry, and in their squat, simple Greek Doric style, embodying a sense of massive solidity and repose. It is the lack of fussiness that appeals.

In his *Memorials* (1873) of Liverpool, the historian J. A. Picton says of Hartley that he was of

> large build and powerful frame, rough in manner and occasionally even rude, using expletives which the angel of mercy would not like to record; sometimes capricious and tyrannical, but occasionally where he was attacked, a firm and unswerving friend. Professionally he had grand ideas and carried them into execution with great strength, solidity and skill which have never been exceeded. Granite was the material in which he delighted to work. His walls are built with rough Cyclopean masses, the face dressed, but otherwise shapeless as from the quarry, cemented with a hydraulic lime of a consistency as hard as the granite itself.

Had granite not existed it would have been necessary to invent it for the particular use of Jesse Hartley.

Cast iron was another characteristic building material of Victorian Liverpool and Quentin Hughes' *Seaport* (1964) – another essential book for anyone interested in Liverpool's architecture – contains excellent descriptions of the buildings which made use of this material. Some of the triumphs in the medium, such as the Sailors' Home, built in 1845 by John Cunningham, have been demolished in the all too recent past. But Liverpool today is in the grip of the heritage mania and for what remains the future is surely secure.

A city that sometimes seems, to the arriving stranger, to have turned its back on the sea, still needs to find a way to reconnect itself more directly and immediately with that magnificent waterfront. Perhaps this will be one outcome of its 'Capital of Culture' status.

A Statue Exceedingly Bare

Liverpool's two modern cathe-
drals – both completed in the twentieth century but as different
architecturally as chalk and cheese – are connected by a street
called Hope: a rather pat connection that has seldom been
overlooked by journalists and caption-writers. These days,
with falling trade in the pews, members of the ecclesiastical
chamber of commerce have to work together to fill their
churches (the real point, perhaps, of ecumenism). Many of
the suburban churches – like St Thomas's in Waterloo where
I would creep through the cold morning streets to serve Mass
and chant the Latin responses – which used to have several
crowded Masses a day on Sunday are now, I learn, combining
with others in the same way as those group parishes of rural
England, where ancient churches in the sleepy shires host
their tiny congregations in rotation. The Anglican and Roman
Catholic Bishop and Archbishop of Liverpool, past rivalries
and antagonisms forgotten, are the best of mates these days.

Liverpool's Metropolitan Cathedral of Christ the King
('Paddy's Wigwam'), designed by Frederick Gibberd and
completed in 1967, was the first cathedral in Britain to be

built in the round. In Anthony Burgess's posthumously published verse novel *Byrne* (1995) it is referred to as 'the massive polyhedral/Holy of holies, Liverpool Cathedral'. When it opened, we were bussed in from the schools to see it and I have never forgotten the impression it made, of newness and modernity and light. Up till then churches had been to me dark places with odd smells, antique heating pipes under grilles, varnished wood pews, spluttering wax votive candles, naff stained glass, pious women in black lace veils mumbling over their rosary beads, and masses of kitsch statuary. But the new cathedral was a shimmering idea of what modern architecture could be. The word was: different. The Anglican cathedral, by contrast, was in the repro and retro tradition, the last flowering of the Gothic revival, and the work of a lifetime for its architect, Giles Gilbert Scott. Like St George's Hall, you have to admire it even if it isn't to your taste: it's a perfect example of its kind and architectural historians such as Joseph Sharples are within their rights to call it 'one of the great buildings of the twentieth century'. Started in 1904, it wasn't actually finished until 1978. Built out of the local red sandstone and occupying a splendid site it is undoubtedly impressive and commanding.

A rather plodding Liverpool folk song that used to be popular in the sixties, 'In My Liverpool Home', contained the refrain 'We speak with an accent exceedingly rare/If you want a Cathedral we've got one to spare/We meet under a statue exceedingly bare/In my Liverpool home'. I've probably got those deathless lines in the wrong order but you get the point. The bare bronze statue is fixed to the front of Lewis's department store on the corner of Renshaw Street and Ranelagh Street and was designed by Jacob Epstein in 1954 to adorn the rebuilt post-war store, the earlier one having been destroyed in the Blitz. It was given the grand title *The Spirit of Liverpool*

Resurgent but it was the genitalia of the heroic figure which attracted most attention and ribaldry.

'We deliberately set ourselves the task of "democratising luxury"', the founder of Lewis's, David Lewis, later said and, like Owen Owen, another department store pioneer, he managed to combine profit with a sense that he was in a way a social pioneer. His name sounds Welsh – drapers and milkmen in English cities at that period often turning out to be Welsh – but David Lewis had changed his name and was in fact the son of a London Jewish merchant called Wolfe Levy. He would later open the Bon Marché store in Church Street where my maternal grandfather, John McElroy, would start his career as a uniformed commissionaire at the door, before working his way up to become a warehouse manager at Arbuckle Smith on Derby Road, Bootle.

John McElroy rose in the firm and was eventually taken to work each day from the company-owned house at Lime Grove, Seaforth, in a chauffeur-driven car. For the first quarter of the twentieth century he was Secretary of the Kirkdale Branch of the Ancient Order of Hibernians until he suddenly parted company, in unexplained circumstances, with the Irish organisation. In his time he had helped to raise money for food parcels for the Irish prisoners in North Wales in the wake of the 1916 Easter Rising. He had a signed photograph from the Irish nationalist MP Major John Redmond and knew the Liverpool Irish MP T. P. O'Connor. A Liberal and a good Catholic, he resented the call by the Liverpool Archbishop Downey in 1929 for all Catholics in the city to vote Labour in order to secure funding for Catholic schools. Dutifully, but resentfully, he voted Labour for the only time in his life. He seems to have been a neat and punctilious man (he died in the year of my birth so I have no recollection of him) who carefully brushed his bowler hat every morning, kept his stiff collars in a round leather box and deplored slovenly behaviour at the warehouse, where men with their hands in their pockets would be reprimanded.

Owen Owen was a real Welshman and was born in the Llyfnant Valley south of Machynlleth in Montgomeryshire. After a spell at his uncle's shop in Bath, learning the ropes, Owen Owen arrived in Liverpool in February 1868 and settled in North View, Edgehill. He soon opened his first shop in 121 London Road. He was ambitious and single-minded – as the seven commandments he drew up for himself indicate. He called these 'a few rules to guide me to the Harbour of Best Success' and they included: '1. Rise very early, and live very well and cheaply... 2. Work myself and be as much as possible in the shop. Help, hands, for I have no lands... 7. Do not frequent theatres, music halls or anything to neglect the business.' Owen Owen was obsessed with detail, with every item in the shop being clearly labelled and staff mustered every morning for a military-style inspection. His business plan was simple: to undercut every competitor and ensure a rapid turnover. An advertising slogan of the time said 'OWEN OWEN/The best article at the lowest price'. But he also cared for his staff. Every year, from 1880 onwards, the company held a 'workpeople's tea party and ball' during January which he paid for out of his own pocket. He was a pioneer of shorter working hours and the first to introduce a weekly half-day holiday well before the 1912 Shops Act made provision for it. He supported Welsh organisations and made donations to the National Eisteddfod and was a stalwart of his local chapel, renting pew No. 105 at the Wesleyan Chapel in Moss Street. Many of his staff were Liverpool Welsh. He was a Liberal in politics and a friend of Lloyd George with links to the London Welsh organisations. He became more and more involved with business and property dealings in the capital, moving to

London in 1893 and using the Adelphi Hotel on his frequent visits to Liverpool. In 1896 he bought a large country house at Penmaenmawr and in 1906 he bought back the family farm at Bwlch which his father had been forced to sell in 1841.

Owen Owen's store in Liverpool was the biggest in the North of England. The store had a floorwalker immaculately dressed in a tailcoat and striped trousers who would conduct the customers to the required department and then draw up chairs for them to sit in while the transactions were carried out. In wet weather one of the many pageboys on duty would shelter the patrons as they approached the main doors and guard umbrellas until the customer's return. Salesgirls in long black frocks stood behind long polished counters and the store was noted for its good silk sold by the yard.

David Lewis was a showman as well as a shopkeeper but he, too, saw himself as a pioneer, creating a wholly new kind of shop. He opened his first store in 1856 and the Bon Marché in 1898, explicitly modelled on the Paris example. Advertising was a key element in creating his brand image and one of his stunts was to issue in December 1882 a series of 'Penny Readings' consisting of 'Selections from the Best Poets, Prose Writers and Best Speakers, together with Miscellaneous and Original Literary Compositions'. More than a quarter of a million of these pamphlets sold in the first eleven weeks and three more editions were produced between 1882 and 1912, the total sale eventually reaching three and a half million. Mindful of his responsibilities to high Victorian decency, Lewis promised that in compiling the readings 'the most assiduous care was taken that no word should appear that would serve as an apology for vice and bring a blush to the cheek of modesty'. Moreover, each copy of the readings was intended to be 'a lesson in THRIFT... a reminder of the price of the People's Penny. Nobody knows what a penny

116

can do until he discovers for himself its enormous power, if rightly expended. "Take care of the pence," said Franklin, "and the pounds will take care of themselves". The proverb is as true today as at the moment it was penned.' As the historian of Lewis's, Asa Briggs, puts it: 'There is no better evidence than these two "morals" of the link between retailing and the "spirit of the age". Respectability and thrift were favourite Victorian virtues, and Lewis could even win profits as well as prestige from the sale of cheap copies of the classics in Liverpool, Manchester, and Birmingham.'

Lewis's boldest and most controversial piece of showmanship was the chartering of the *Great Eastern* in 1886 to coincide with an International Exhibition of Navigation, Travelling, Commerce and Manufactures. It was opened by Queen Victoria herself. On the starboard side of the famous ship it was announced that Lewis's stores were THE FRIENDS OF THE PEOPLE and on the port side LADIES SHOULD VISIT THE BON MARCHE, CHURCH STREET. Three million people visited the Liverpool exhibition, of whom 20,000 went aboard the *Great Eastern* over four days. Between April and October, when the boat remained, visitor numbers exceeded half a million. But there were some in Liverpool who saw this as a vulgar stunt, offensive to the great maritime traditions of the port. This, they felt, was a great record-breaking vessel which had been turned by a shopkeeper into a gaudy sideshow.

A great many famous ships like the *Great Eastern* have passed through the Mersey. But by the end of the 1960s the port's passenger supremacy was over and liners started to sail instead from Southampton. I have already mentioned the great white Canadian Pacific liners which I watched as a child. Just before Christmas 1971, the great Italian writer Primo Levi was in Liverpool on a business trip (he worked all his life as an industrial chemist) and he went down to the docks to watch what was probably the last of these transatlantic liners, the *Empress of Canada*, leave on her farewell voyage to the scrapyard at Tilbury, saluted by boats on the Mersey. I think I, too, may have watched this sad departure as a schoolboy from our windows at Waterloo.

Not everyone, however, was bowled over by the famous boats. Francis Kilvert, the diarist, paid a visit to Liverpool on 30th June 1872, in the course of which he went on board the Cunard liner *Batavia*: 'I was appalled at the smallness and darkness of the first class cabins'. He was also disappointed in another great ship, the *Great Britain*: 'She was painted black and white and looked like a collier beside the modern huge steamships'. He was more impressed by the Laird ship-building works on the other side of the river at Birkenhead, from whose slips the *Alabama* had been launched, and by the Sailors' Home ('a capital place').

Kilvert arrived at the Liverpool Landing Stage on a ferry from Birkenhead on Wednesday 19th June 1872, having come from his home in the Welsh Marches, via the train from Wrexham to Chester. Typically, he became engrossed by 'two merry saucy Irish hawking girls' who were with him on the train. He caught a hansom cab at the Landing Stage to visit his hosts in Everton. From there, '[we] went to the Exchange, one of the finest buildings of the kind in the world, and passing upstairs into the gallery and leaning upon the broad marble ledge we looked down upon a crowd of merchants and brokers swarming and humming like a hive of bees in the floor of the vast area below'. All around the enormous hall, as Kilvert looked down, were 'desks or screens or easels or huge slates covered with the latest telegrams, notices of London stock and share lists, cargoes, freights, sales, outward and homebound ships, times of sailing, states of wind and weather, barometer readings'. The quadrangle outside is called Exchange Flags,

24 Tom Mann (1856–1941) addressing striking workers during the 1911 transport strike (LVRO)

25 Eric Heffer (1922–1991), MP for Walton, at the Labour Party Conference, 1986 (© Hulton Deutsch Collection/Corbis)

26 Bessie Braddock (1899–1970), MP for Liverpool Exchange, dancing with Frankie Vaughan at the Labour Party Conference, 1963

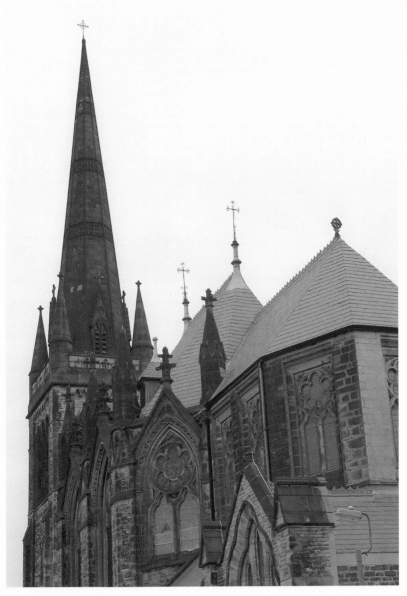

27 St Francis Xavier's church, Everton (© Dave Wood www.liverpoolpictorial..
co.uk)

28 Siegfried Sassoon (1886–1967), 1915 (© Hulton Deutsch Collection/Corbis)

29 Sand dunes at Formby (© NT/E. Chambré Hardman Collection)

30 Overhead Railway and the Dock Road, with Princes Dock in the background (© NT/E. Chambré Hardman Collection)

31 Princes Dock, 1981 (LVRO)

32 Karel Capek (1890–1938), left, with his brother Joseph, 1938 (© Bettmann/ Corbis)

33 George Orwell (1903–1950) (© Bettmann/Corbis)

34 J. B. Priestley (1894–1984), 1941 (© Hulton Deutsch Collection/Corbis)

35 St Nicholas Church (© Brian Saville)

36 Stuart Sutcliffe (1940–1962) (© Bettmann/Corbis)

37 Philharmonic Hotel, Hope Street, interior

38 The Crown, Lime Street

39 The Liverpool Poets, painted by Peter Edwards (1985) (© National Portrait Gallery, London)

40 Fritz Spiegl (1926–2003) (private collection © Ingrid Spiegl)

41 Edward Chambré Hardman (1898–1988), photographer, in uniform
(© NT/ E. Chambré Hardman Collection)

42 Exchange Flags, 1935 (© NT/ E.Chambré Hardman Collection)

43 Liverpool Cathedral, 1950 (© NT/E. Chambré Hardman Collection)

44 Metropolitan Cathedral and Hope Street (© NT/E. Chambré Hardman Collection)

45 School for the Blind, Hope Street, 1931 (© NT/E. Chambré Hardman Collection)

46 Playhouse Theatre, 1972 (© NT/E. Chambré Hardman Collection)

47 The Blackie Arts Centre and the Chinese Arch, Nelson Street (the author)

where the cotton merchants met. Kilvert noted how the pavement was white with the fluff of cotton samples.

The next day Kilvert set off on a steamboat for New Brighton across the Mersey:

> The morning was lovely, all was fresh and new, the salt air and the wind exhilarating and I was in dancing spirits. The Mersey was gay and almost crowded with vessels of all sorts moving up and down the river, ships, barques, brigs, brigantines, schooners, cutters, colliers, tugs, steamboats, lighters, 'flats', everything from the huge emigrant liner steamship with four masts to the tiny sailing and rowing boat. From the river one sees to advantage the miles of docks which line the Mersey side, and the forests of masts which crowd the quays, 'the pine forest of the sea, mast and spar'.

Kilvert's joyful enthusiasm is a welcome contrast to Hawthorne's gloomy excursion up the same stretch of river twenty years earlier. Not that he was ignoring the harsher realities such as the teeming emigrant ships: 'They seemed crowded with Irish and German emigrants and small steamboats kept bringing fresh loads of passengers alongside the big ships. One could not help thinking of the hundreds of sorrowful hearts on board and ashore and the farewells and partings for ever, so many of them, on this side of the grave.' Kilvert was also enthused by the docks:

> Nothing gives one so vivid an idea of the vast commerce of the country as these docks, quays and immense warehouses, piled and cumbered with hides, cotton, tallow, corn, oilcake, wood and wine, oranges and other fruit and merchandize of all kinds from all corners of the world. I admired the dray horses very much, huge creatures 17 or 18 hands high, more like elephants than horses. Liverpool boasts the finest breed of Flemish draught horse in the world.

Kilvert saw Liverpool in its mercantile prime, the second port of Empire, with its vast disparities of wealth and opportunity: 'Liverpool left upon my mind an impression of ragged Irish bare-footed women and children. Enormous wealth and squalid poverty, wildernesses of offices and palatial counting-houses and warehouses, bustling pushing vulgar men, pretty women and lovely children.'

The following year the French writer Hippolyte Taine arrived in Liverpool and, as already noted, found the Irish quarter 'the lowest circle of hell'. The situation of the port in a 'flat and sodden land' – those soggy 'mosses' of south-west Lancashire which proved such a nightmare for the early railway builders – was, according to Taine, 'made for wild duck rather than men'. The dyspeptic Frenchman was profoundly unimpressed by the triumph of St George's Hall: 'a sort of temple with a gilded ceiling and columns of imitation jasper. It is a concert hall, with a horribly crude organ making a hideous row inside'. There was, he concluded, 'no point in seeking beauty and elegance here. Liverpool, like Manchester, is a monster: monumental counting-houses and warehouses, immense streets of houses overburdened, as in London, with arcades, columns and pilasters, whose sole effect on the spectator is to leave him with an impression of overwhelming clutter'. One thing that did impress Taine, as it impressed every other foreign visitor, was the extent of the docks. He noted the 'cyclopean rampart' of the cotton warehouses alongside the docks, and the dock basins themselves which 'put one in mind of rectangular, aquatic streets multiplied and ramified into a whole town'. And the ships: 'their crowded masts appear like a leafless, winter-bound forest extending as far as the eye can see and barring the whole horizon to the north... The spectacle of the Liverpool docks is, I think, one of the greatest in the whole world.'

Taine was impressed by the sheer bulk of the ships like the *Great Britain*, which was about to sail for Australia with twelve hundred emigrants: 'If you go down the steps of a dry dock to the level of the ship's keel, you realise that the hull of a ship is forty or fifty feet tall. The vessel's swelling flanks, covered with copper sheeting, have the gracious lines of a wild-fowl asleep upon the waves.' From Birkenhead, Taine had a fine view of Liverpool and the Mersey in 1873:

> From Birkenhead one can see the whole port across the enormous spread of the river; its yellow-gleaming surface is almost flat calm under the light mist. Steam-boats wallow up and down stream, meet and pass, with a stiff, mechanical motion, like black crabs. Sailing-ships glide down the river, bowing, supple, beautiful as swans. The ninety-gun man-o'-war *George*, with both sails and steam, arrives in harbour like a sovereign, all that crowd of shipping making way for her. On the far shore the endless line of masts and rigging bristles against the sky, behind it the colossal heap of the town.

Taine felt surrounded everywhere he went by the same impression: what he called 'enormousness'. But this could not dispel the other overwhelming fact about nineteenth-century Liverpool:

> In the neighbourhood of Leeds Street there are fifteen or twenty streets with ropes stretched across them where rags and underwear were hung out to dry. Every stairway swarms with children, five or six to a step, the eldest nursing the baby; their faces are pale, their hair whitish and tousled, the rags they wear full of holes, they have neither shoes nor stockings and they are all vilely dirty. Their faces and limbs seemed to be encrusted with dust and soot. In one street alone there must have been about two hundred children sprawling and fighting... What rooms! A threadbare

slip of oilcloth on the floor, sometimes a big sea-shell or one or two plaster ornaments; the old, idiot grandmother crouches in one corner; the wife is engaged in trying to mend some wretched rags of clothes; the children tumble over each other. The smell is that of an old-clothes shop full of rotting rags... Some of the tiniest children are still fresh and rosy-cheeked, but it hurts to look at their great blue eyes; for that clear, healthy blood is going to be spoilt; as they grow older they become etiolated, their flesh becomes flabby and unwholesomely livid, and you can see scrofulous little faces marred by small open sores covered with a piece of paper.

A detail which Taine found particularly 'horrible' was the fact that many of the streets in which these wretched people lived were quite regular and relatively new, the product of municipal intervention: 'so that this was an example of the best that can be done for the poor'. Rembrandt's beggars, Taine concluded, 'were happier and better off in their picturesque hovels'.

Kilvert and Taine admired both the ships on the river and the shipbuilding works on the Birkenhead side that had become by the time of my childhood Cammell Laird's, where one of my uncles worked, having fitted wireless systems to some famous Cunard boats. One of the most memorable images of modern British photography, Edward Chambré Hardman's *The Birth of the Ark Royal*, captures, in 1950, the vast aircraft carrier, painted white for its launch, and seeming to hover, ghost-like, over the terraces of Birkenhead while in the foreground a boy with a satchel over his shoulder and a cap walks quietly towards it down the middle of an empty street.

Hardman was an Irishman, born in Dublin in 1898, the son of an amateur photographer whose equipment Edward started to experiment with as a child. In 1917, when his father died, Hardman joined the army and was eventually commissioned in the Gurkha Rifles. Hardman returned from India in 1922 with a fellow officer, Kenneth Burrell, to establish a portrait studio business in Liverpool which became his home for the rest of his life. Central to his life and his business was his wife Margaret Mills, who was also a photographer. Burrell and Hardman established a studio in Bold Street in 1923 which became very fashionable. Hardman photographed various rising actors, including Robert Donat, Michael Redgrave and a young actress from the Liverpool Playhouse called Beryl Bainbridge. In 1948 Hardman moved to the grander location of 59 Rodney Street where he lived over the studio for the rest of his life. He died in 1988, devastated by the death of his wife in 1970, and having come to the attention of social services in 1979 as an elderly man living on his own in a large Georgian house unable to climb the stairs. Social workers alerted a local photography gallery, the Open Eye Gallery, to the house and its contents, and Hardman was persuaded by its director, Peter Hagerty, to establish a trust to ensure the survival of the collection. After Hardman's death in 1988 the house and its contents were acquired by the National Trust and it was recently opened to the public complete with restored 1950s' furniture, the photographic archive of 140,000 negatives itself stored under special conditions in the Liverpool Record Office.

One other famous ship, the *Titanic*, was, like so many of the great liners, registered (though not actually built) in Liverpool. When the ship goes down, in the 1997 movie of that name, the last words seen on the stern as the boat finally disappears beneath the waves are TITANIC/LIVERPOOL.

123

12

Of All Places the Most Museless

A fondness for words – odd, quirky, archaic words – was one of the characteristics of my father, a Liverpool primary school headmaster whose logophilia occasionally went, naturally enough, with a schoolmaster's pedantic streak. Like many Liverpudlians he was an ardent student of the *Liverpool Echo*, and I remember one day his tapping the paper irritably, having discovered a spelling that disagreed with him. He had been running his eye down the small advertisements placed by various obscure pop groups playing at city centre clubs like the Cavern, and he had spotted an advertisement for one of the as yet unknown bands. 'Look at how they have spelled their name,' he announced disapprovingly: 'The *Beatles*!!'

I preferred his logophilia to his pedantry. 'Stop standing there like a pilgarlick!' he would say to us. Although I think I know what he meant, I have never established what a pilgarlick is. It would be a simple matter of reaching for the *Oxford English Dictionary* but I feel that I decided long ago what it meant and it would spoil the fun to be told something else by a lexical authority. He also referred to as a W.C. as a 'ginty'

– or was it 'jinty'? Sometimes his verbal snatches were from the pages of the *Golden Treasury* – a favourite was Browning's 'Soliloquy of the Spanish Cloister' where the pointless chatter of the monks is captured ('Not a plenteous cork crop: scarcely/Dare we hope oak-galls, I doubt'). At other times he would whimsically recall the titles of (possibly apocryphal) books, such as *Every Man His Own Farrier*. What on earth was a farrier? A question that could be answered quickly, I am told, by any horsey girl from Surrey, but to a 1960s' Liverpool urban schoolboy it was not a word in currency.

Later, I would fall in love with the poetry of Gerard Manley Hopkins and its magnificent verbal music, its splendid disregard for the tidy proprieties of English verse. And I would fall in love with one poem in particular: 'Felix Randal': 'Felix Randal, the farrier, O is he dead then?'. Its sonorous ending thrilled me and thrills me still, like the clashing of some great metal door, wonderfully perverse and clangorous in its diction, gloriously alliterative: 'Didst fettle for the great grey drayhorse his bright and battering sandal!'

Much later, when I sat down to study this poem as an undergraduate, I would discover that the subject of the poem was a Scouser and its author a curate at a Liverpool parish.

Father Gerard Manley Hopkins, SJ, arrived in Liverpool at the very end of 1879 to take up an appointment as one of the curates at St Francis Xavier's parish in Salisbury Street, not far from the city centre. Just round the corner was a row of very scruffy and neglected Georgian houses – now shimmeringly restored – in Shaw Street. At around the time I fell in love with the poetry of Hopkins I also fell in love with a young student who lived in the middle of this row, at the top of a house owned by a doctor whose surgery was on the ground floor. At night mice would come out to play, sometimes scurrying across her coverlet. I was a good Catholic boy in those days so I was never present at their nocturnal outings but when I walked down Shaw Street recently, admiring the restoration, I couldn't help wondering where all the mice had gone. I am surer about the fate of the owner of that coverlet. She is my wife.

Hopkins had arrived, around the corner, from a parish in Leigh in Lancashire, where he had become very fond of the people, seduced by what he told his friend Robert Bridges was 'the charming and cheery heartiness of these Lancashire Catholics, which is deeply comforting'. Liverpool, however, gave him no comfort. After four months in the job he wrote to another friend, Alexander Baillie: 'My Liverpool work is very harassing and makes it hard to write. Tonight I am sitting in my confessional, but the faithful are fewer than usual... Here comes someone.' To another friend in the same month, Hopkins confessed: 'The parish work of Liverpool is very wearying to mind and body and leaves me with nothing but odds and ends of time. There is merit in it but little Muse, and indeed 26 lines is the whole I have written in more than half a year, since I left Oxford.' By the end of 1880 things were no better. He confessed to Richard Watson Dixon: 'Liverpool is of all places the most museless. It is indeed a most unhappy and miserable spot. There is moreover no time for writing anything serious.'

Hopkins had indeed written very little but that little was to include one of the greatest short lyrics in English of the nineteenth century. On 21st April 1880 a 31-year-old horse-shoer or farrier, Felix Spencer, died of consumption in his Birchfield street home in the parish. He had been visited on his death-bed by Father Hopkins. Seven days later Hopkins wrote his poem about a man whose death meant that 'my duty all ended'. Into the poem Hopkins (a logophile like my father) slipped in a Lancashire expression ('all road' =

everyone). He had recently told one of his Oxford friends that '[the] common people of this town talk of "a little weany bit"', and again had noted on a reluctant visit to a church bazaar at St Helens the colourful phrasing of a man called Mr Derby who tried to persuade Hopkins to come out riding with him. If he did so, Derby promised, he would 'make [your] lip curl like a bee's knee in a gale of wind'.

Hopkins was touched by the tears of the dying young man ('Thy tears that touched my heart, child, Felix, poor Felix Randal') and contrasted the farrier's consumption with the vigour of his early manhood: 'How far from then fore-thought of, all thy more boisterous years,/When thou at the random grim forge, powerful amidst peers,/Didst fettle for the great drayhorse his bright and battering sandal!' In June, the poet sent to Bridges 'a sonnet and a little lyric' ('Felix Randal' and 'At a Wedding'), saying they were 'the only things I have written in nine months'.

I sometimes reflect that my great-grandfather, William Murray, was working in Liverpool in a forge at the same time as Felix Spencer, and could have known him – but this was a common profession, shoeing all those tall drayhorses observed by Kilvert and the other Victorian visitors to the city.

From time to time Hopkins would escape the misery of 'SFX' for the beauty of the Lancashire countryside. Rose Hill, Lydiate, was the home of a man called Randall Lightbound, a devout Catholic with a private chapel attached to his country house which was served by the Jesuits from Salisbury Street. The proximity of 'Randall' to 'Randal' is presumably not acci-dental. Each week, in rotation, one of the curates would go to Rose Hill to say Mass and, in September 1880, walking back to the station, Hopkins composed another short and sadly beau-tiful lyric, 'Spring and Fall', provoked by the autumn leaves: 'Margaret, are you grieving/Over Goldengrove unleaving…'

Museless, Liverpool may have seemed, but it was a far from barren period if it could produce poems of this order.

Early in 1881, Hopkins took a walk out of Liverpool eastwards in the direction of the Lancashire hinterland. He had left before dawn on foot 'by frost and starlight' through frozen drifts of deep snow but soon lost his way at a place called Gillmoss, where two children fetching milk said to the priest (in his phonetic rendering to Robert Bridges) 'You must follow ooz.' These sound like Lancashire kids but today Gillmoss is a tough district radically altered in the 1950s by Liverpool Corporation's policy of 'overspill', which also created the better known Kirkby – the setting of the 1960s' TV police series *Z Cars*. Now Scouse accents rather than Lancastrian ones predominate. In 1956 a new headmaster arrived at the Catholic primary school, St Swithin's, which, given the zeal with which the policy of decanting families from the inner Liverpool slums was pursued, became briefly the largest junior school in the UK, the jerry-built structure bursting with new admissions. In addition to being headmaster, my father also found himself carrying plastic buckets to school on the back of his motorbike to catch the drips. I have written about this elsewhere (in my novel *A Short Book About Love*) but that rotten building seemed to stand for the worst kind of post-war British architecture. Moreover, the whole 'overspill' experiment in social engineering seems, at the least, questionable. Refurbishment of the inner Liverpool housing stock and infrastructure (the sort of thing private developers with an eye to young urban professionals get involved in) might have had happier results, building on existing and latent community strengths.

It was cold that January of 1881. A couple of days later Hopkins went down to the Mersey to see the ice on the river and to check out the 'infinite flocks of seagulls' of which he had been told. I recall only once in my childhood seeing the Mersey frozen in this way:

> The river was coated with dirty yellow ice from shore to shore; where the edges could be seen it seemed very thick; it was not smooth but many broken pieces framed or pasted together again; it was floating down stream with the ebb tide; it everywhere covered the water, but was not of a piece, being continually broken, ploughed up by the plying of the steam ferryboats, which I believe sometimes can scarcely make their way across. The gulls were pampered; throngs of people were chucking them bread.

When it came to the human scene, Hopkins was another outsider, another appalled observer of the urban squalor of nineteenth-century Liverpool, but his recoil seems to have been as much a moral as an aesthetic one: there seemed to him something vicious in the aspect of the people around him. After a May Day procession in Liverpool in 1881 during which he had admired the handsome horses, he noted 'for the thousandth time with sorrow and loathing the base and bespotted figures and features of the Liverpool crowd'. This echoed an earlier comment written in a letter from the rural sanctuary of Rose Hill, Lydiate: 'human nature is so inveterate. Would that I had seen the last of it'. Hopkins, in the confessional, and in his daily rounds, saw a great deal of human misery, to which (as is clear from 'Felix Randal') he was sympathetic and sensitive, but he also saw the 'vice' to which he was not. He had a brief escape in June 1881 to Oxford, where for a time he felt, like the people of Euripides, that he could say 'I see the sun'. Back in Liverpool he wrote to his Oxford friend, Francis de Paravicini: 'Now at Liverpool one can *not* see the sun. Not but what for Liverpool, too, "hellhole" though it is, something can be said.'

129

Hopkins left Liverpool early in 1882 for Glasgow which, oddly enough, he found more sympathetic, especially its Irish community. Writing to his mother on New Year's Day 1882 while out of Liverpool on leave, he reported: 'One of our Fathers, who was for the best part of two years my yokemate on that laborious mission, died there yesterday night after a short sickness, in harness and in his prime. I am saddened by his death, for he was particularly good to me; he used to come up to me and say "Gerard, you are a good soul" and that I was a comfort to him in his troubles.'

Another reluctant Oxford clerical visitor, educated as a child at St Francis Xavier's ('I found it a dark, frightening place') was Anthony Kenny, who arrived at the church of the Sacred Heart in Liverpool 8 as a curate in September 1959. The archbishop of Liverpool, Cardinal John Heenan, had told him that after Oxford he needed a taste of parish life: 'I am sure that in the immediate future you will benefit spiritually by working in a parish'. Kenny – today a laicised Oxford philosopher – found this district of central Liverpool 'depressed and depressing'. He also felt uncomfortable at the luxury enjoyed by the clergy – good food and wine in a sea of urban deprivation. One of the curate's duties was to pay house calls to collect money from the parishioners, half of whom lived in substandard housing conditions or in flats built to replace the slums in which they lived 'often equally discontented'. Everyone had, as he put it, 'lost families or neighbours who had been rehoused in outlying suburbs like Kirkby' – or Gillmoss. In a striking echo of Hopkins, Kenny wrote in his autobiography, *A Path From Rome*: 'The years at Sacred Heart were among the most depressing of my life... I was lonely and felt starved of congenial company.'

Liverpool does not seem promising territory for Oxford men, in spite of all those streets named after its colleges.

Kenny later became Master of Balliol in the 1980s. This was a decade in which the very ordinary north Liverpool suburb in which I grew up, and to which Kenny moved after his spell at Sacred Heart, and where I remember him from schooldays, provided Britain with not just the Master of Balliol but also the Director General of the BBC and the Archbishop of Canterbury, all three men serving more or less at the same time in these key Establishment posts, and all from working-class or lower-middle-class backgrounds. At the time of writing it has delivered up the serving General Secretary of the Trades Union Congress, Brendan Barber. I remember his being in the year above me at school, a fact of which I reminded him at a party at the Foreign Office to celebrate the 90th birthday of Michael Foot. I should say that I do not normally move in such elite circles – my wife and I had won two tickets to the event in the *Tribune* readers' raffle. Barber is an amiable and easygoing chap without any side but was, perhaps understandably, distinctly underwhelmed by my news.

Our last voice from the nineteenth century is that of the Reverend R. A. Armstrong, author of *The Deadly Shame of Liverpool*, whose sermon preached on 22nd May 1892 at his Hope Street Church is too good to be passed over. It was entitled 'The Call of God to the Middle Classes of England'. God's call was to save England from the dark whirlpool of vice into which it was being sucked. With the swinish proles on the one hand, and on the other the decadent upper classes, the God-fearing middle classes, bound in the armour of righteousness, heroically strode up Hope Street to save their country. These were the people whose self-satisfied smugness and philistinism had been satirised and challenged by Matthew Arnold, who, four years earlier, had died suddenly in Liverpool of a heart attack.

Arnold was in Liverpool to meet the transatlantic liner

Aurania, which contained his daughter Lucy, her husband and her daughter, Eleanor. Arnold and his wife were staying at Dingle Bank, a large house next to the Mersey, where his younger sister Lucy and her husband John Cropper – descendant of the anti-slavery campaigner James Cropper – now lived. On the fine Saturday evening, 14th April 1888, Arnold went for a walk, leaping gaily over a set of low railings in his high-spirited anticipation of Lucy's arrival. The next day, receiving news that the *Aurania* had docked, he set off briskly along Dingle Lane to catch a tram to the docks when he fell forward and collapsed just outside the old Toxteth chapel. Opposite was a doctor's house into which he was carried but he was pronounced dead at 2.45 pm. At 9.45 am on Tuesday 17th April the coffin was placed in a closed hearse and driven to Lime Street Station where a clergyman with the beguiling name of Reverend J. T. Slugg was waiting to receive the body. Four railway porters carried the coffin to the brake van at the back of the saloon attached to the 11.05 London train, stopping briefly at Edge Hill to collect Arnold's wife and family.

Arriving at Liverpool I always think of that brief pause and pick-up as the train slows at Edge Hill before plunging into the high sandstone tunnel which dramatically takes one into Lime Street.

When the Reverend Armstrong mounted his pulpit on that May morning in Liverpool he announced that there were 'many terrible facts about the vices and crimes of the poor, which lead some of us to shudder at them' but in fairness there were also 'a few terrible facts about the vices and crimes of the rich, which some of us pass over'. He flattered his congregation that even if they were to be 'herded in the slums of Scotland Road, with the flashing gin palaces all around', their titanic moral strength would protect them. They would never 'fall into drink and crime'. On the other hand, if they belonged to the ranks of the idle rich of the 'smart sets' then they would most certainly plunge headlong into the moral mire:

> But it is for us, the great middle class of England, from the skilled artisan or the patient clerk to the merchant or the professional man who prospers but still has to practise his economies, – it is for us, this great middle class of England to recognise that to us with our education, our refinement, our moderate estate, our immunities from great temptations, comes the call of God to be the saving force of England. It is on us the divine voice calls so to steer this ancient and beloved commonwealth that it shall not go down in a black flood of vice, but shall through centuries yet unborn still stand before the world for manly industry, for probity, for freedom, for domestic purity, for pure and sweet religion. It is these things that are threatened by wealthy and aristocratic vice.

Armstrong's regimen for those thus called upon to steer the ship of righteousness through the black storm of vice was '[s]implicity in food, in dress, in recreation, habitual service of their fellows and kindly human helpfulness, the love of the poor and weak and hapless, these must you make the manners of your own and you children's daily life'.

Excellent principles but ones that sit uneasily with the rousing denunciations of those very 'poor and weak and hapless' in the slums of Scotland Road.

13

White Lace on Dark Waters

On Wednesday 29th March, 1905, Virginia Stephen (later Virginia Woolf) arrived in Liverpool at around 2.30 in the afternoon. She had caught the 10.45 am train from Euston, a journey (if one is lucky) made considerably shorter today. She caught a bus to the Pier Head where a great crowd was gathered, bustling with farewells and preparations. Woolf was in Liverpool to embark as one of the 140 first-class passengers on the Booth Line steamship *Anselm* for France but there were bigger ships and grander destinations being prepared down at the Pier Head. 'A huge steamer, the *Oceanic*, second largest afloat,' she wrote in her diary, 'was black with passengers, just leaving for America.' Her own boat was 'all white & clean and luxurious' and soon she was heading down the Mersey for France: 'We walked on the deck & saw all the lights along the Coast of Wales, steamers passing, & our own foam spread like white lace on the dark waters – a very lovely thing is a ship at sea.'

Woolf was one of a long line of visitors to Liverpool who came solely for the purpose of taking to the sea, and who probably saw very little else of the city, catching, as she did,

134

a bus or a cab from Lime Street Station to the Pier Head.
That traffic is ended now and the typically featureless airport
terminal has deprived the transatlantic traveller of a great deal
of incidental pleasure. Liverpudlians have always been appre-
ciative of the dramatic visual quality of the river and the docks
and when the new Liverpool Overhead Railway was opened
in 1893 one of its selling points was the pleasure to be derived
from its views of the shipping. Virginia Woolf might well have
caught sight of an advertising poster current at the time of her
visit which announced that 'A ROUND TRIP of 13 miles is
the BEST way to see the FINEST DOCKS in the world and the
GIANT OCEAN LINERS'. A first-class ticket for this excursion
was a shilling and third class (there was no second class) was
ninepence. As Liverpool prepares for an influx of tourists in
its year as European Capital of Culture in 2008 there must
be many who wish this railway – closed in 1956 – was still
around. I may have been taken on it as a small child but I
have no recollection of it, though I have vivid memories of
the elevated viaducts which remained in place for a long time
after its closure.

When it opened 'the Over'ead', or 'the Dockers' Umbrella'
as it was known, was the first overhead electric railway in
the world. The New York Elevated Railway – which had been
something of a model – used steam traction, not electricity.
The idea of such a railway was first mooted in 1852 with
an idea of hauling goods and passengers by horse traction
but it wasn't until 1877 that the Mersey Docks and Harbour
Board sent an engineer to New York to study the railway there,
which had been open since 1870. In 1882 a plan for a steam-
operated overhead railway was drawn up and the requisite
Act of Parliament passed, but nothing happened until 1888
when an independent company was formed to construct a
railway from the Alexandra Dock to the Herculaneum Dock,

a distance of just over five miles. The Liverpool Overhead Railway Company was incorporated by an Act on 24th July 1888 and construction began in October 1889. It consisted of a steel viaduct sixteen feet above road level and the trains, originally planned to run on steam, were electric because this was now considered cheaper, with the example of the City and South London Railway to hand.

The first portion of the Overhead Railway was opened on 4th February 1893 by the Marquis of Salisbury. He pushed a button in the plinth of a silver inkstand bearing a border of ship's cables but the resultant growling of the dynamos drowned out the sound of the worthy speeches that followed. The Overhead was the first railway built in the United Kingdom on an iron viaduct, the first worked by an electric current transmitted from a generating station over a system of more than five miles, and the first protected by electric automatic signals. For all these reasons it was seen as a pioneer of city electric railways. Much of its traffic came from dockers using it early in the morning to get to work but, especially with the northern extension in 1894 as far as Seaforth Sands, it aimed to reach out to the residential districts. It was at Seaforth Sands station that in January 1901 what was only the second escalator in the country was installed and this innovation began to feature in publicity for the railway. A 1901 poster advertised the 'Moving Staircase' against a picture of the station, promising 'punctual service of trains every five minutes. Splendid view of six miles of Docks and River Frontage. Special rates for Excursionists. Quickest route to all the Docks, Seaforth, Waterloo and Great Crosby also Prince's and Sefton Parks.' There was a fixed fare of twopence for any distance. Unfortunately, by 1906, the moving staircase had to be abandoned after numerous complaints and claims for compensation from the public after ladies' voluminous skirts had been caught in the exposed moving parts.

In June 1930 a new station was built at Gladstone Dock and gradually the old wooden slatted seats were modernised with the arrival of leather and padded armrests. But by 1954 the system was in need of repair and the company could not afford the £2 million needed, so the decision was taken to close the railway. Within two months of its closure vandalism had been so extensive that the decision was taken to demolish it. H. Maxwell Rostron, the former General Manager and Engineer of the Liverpool Overhead Railway, now a freelance engineer, tendered for the contract to demolish the railway he had managed from 1943 to 1956. Rostron was the son of Captain Sir Arthur Henry Rostron, former Commodore of the Cunard Fleet and in command of the *Carpathia* which came to the rescue of the *Titanic* in April 1912.

What had settled the Overhead's hash was competition from buses and trams (the latter being converted to buses) and a reluctance to invest in the railway's future. In 1959 Rostron observed – in words that have even more force now, delivered as they were before talk of energy crisis and global warming was universal – that

> the majority of ordinary people today, so far as public transport is concerned, are so mesmerised with the diesel bus, that they forget that every drop of fuel for that vehicle has to be imported from not very reliable sources. Furthermore, such liquid fuel is essentially of a limited nature, and the time will come when Merseysiders must rue the day when they permitted the City Fathers to throttle the lifeblood of this unique undertaking, and in addition to scrap the last vestige of their remarkably efficient electric tramway system.

The Liverpool Docks and the waterfront continued to fascinate a range of observers, from the local excursionists on the

Overhead to the more literary imaginations. One of the finest modern writers from Liverpool, James Hanley (1901–85), a writer still insufficiently well known and a remarkably original and inventive talent (those adjectives possibly explaining his neglect in England), whose *Times* obituary was headed 'Neglected Genius of the Novel', was brought up in Liverpool, though born in Dublin. Novels such as *The Ocean* (1941) and *The Last Voyage* (1931) ought to be taken for granted as modern classics but it is unlikely that a copy of any of his books could be found today in Liverpool or that Hanley's name will be celebrated in the city's 'Year of Culture'. In his 1937 'autobiographical excursion', *Broken Water*, there are two passages which evoke something of this side of Liverpool, the way a great seaport gets an imaginative hold on its inhabitants:

> There was plenty of time, so I walked leisurely down the street and on to the road, and so on down the steep hill that took me to the dock road itself. When I reached the bottom I stood for some minutes watching the stream of traffic thundering past. Cars, lorries, dock trains, engines, cabs, taxis, runners' traps, and vans. All the world's goods were passing along that great highway. And there through the gate opposite me I could see the masts of the many ships, hear the familiar rattling sound of their winches, the cries of men, see the working cranes, hear the great noises in the sheds as the ships were loaded or unloaded, the sun shining on it all and making a wonderful picture, the sort of picture that would die on canvas or the printed page.

Hanley then, in an oblique, visionary passage, dreams of writing a book about the city:

> Sometimes when I have walked the pavements I have imagined a kind of rage lurking somewhere beneath the stones,

138

a kind of electric undercurrent running like veins beneath the floor of the great city. I loved walking alone at night, the street lamps lit, the air heavy and perhaps a slight drizzle powdering the pavements, so that there gleamed a strange colour under the yellowish lights, hearing no sounds save that of a single ship's syren far out in the river, and above it the sky an almost angry red reflecting the labours of men far below, the ship growing upon the piles. And from that red sky to look down a narrow street, a long street, its fast shut doors, streams of light issuing from beneath, or from windows here and there, peopling the street with shadows of all shapes and sizes. Streets of adventure every one of them, each with its own history, own atmosphere, own peculiar look in the light of day and in the darkness at night.

Hanley was a controversial writer whose 1931 novel *Boy* was withdrawn as a result of police action when it was reissued in 1934. A man from Bury in Lancashire had taken the book out of the local public library and complained subsequently to the police about its content. Officers descended on the branch library on 27th November 1934, seized the book as obscene and indecent, and the next day issued a summons to the library authorities, as a result of which the book was withdrawn in January 1935 by the publishers. The latter consulted a firm of lawyers retained by the Authors' Society whose view it was that a conviction was likely (the directors of the publishing house and the librarian had been committed to trial at Manchester Assizes for promoting 'an obscene libel...against the Peace of Our Lord the King, his Crown and Dignity'). The lawyers said that it was odd that nobody had perceived this obscenity during the three and a half years since the book's first publication in a limited edition in 1931, but that 'upon this case being tried before a jury in Manchester, that jury will probably consider that it is its duty to vindicate at least the honour of Lancashire'. In the event each director of the company, though they had pleaded guilty and offered to withdraw the book, was fined £50, though the author was never prosecuted. Closing the case the judge, Mr Justice Porter, observed enigmatically: 'It is not for me to discuss the question as to whether there has been an obscene libel or not, but I have my own strong and personal views about it.' The honour of Lancashire had been upheld.

Another important twentieth-century Liverpool writer, George Garrett (1896–1966), greatly admired by George Orwell, also left an autobiographical sketch, still never published in its entirety, called *Ten Years on the Parish*. In this work he paints a portrait of Liverpool docks in 1913, the year of my father's birth, 'with its seven-mile dock road running parallel to the River Mersey, and its elevated street-railway overlooking both'. Garrett describes two long streams of horse-drawn traffic carrying merchandise in opposite directions, to and from the ships:

> To and from them, lumbering along, past warehouses, railway depots, ship repair-yards, and the many gaudy public-houses wedged in between, crawled these two continuous lines of vehicles: wagons and carts of different lengths and shapes; two-wheeled floats, heavy drays and high spring-carts; four-wheeled timber-drags, pony wagons, one-horse wagons, and team-horse wagons; loaded with everything from wet hides to new boots, chocolates to deadly poisons, feathers to marble slabs, and gold ingots to scrap iron.

Long before he left school at the age of thirteen, Garrett got to know the Liverpool docks, meeting his mother outside school to take delivery of his father's lunch, 'which usually consisted of cheese or meat sandwiches, and fivepence, the price of two pints of beer. Off I would dash then to whatever part of the docks my father happened to be working in as a stevedore.' After Garrett left his 'slum elementary school' he went to work as a 'steam-lad' at the cargo winches, where he longed – like so many young Liverpool boys – to go away to sea. He watched the sailors arrive: 'They filled me with wonder as they filed down the gangways holding up parrots, or monkeys, or canaries, or any souvenirs that showed trace of a far-off country. These men were to me somehow a race apart with a gait of their own. Secretly I yearned to be one of them...'

Romantic literature has encouraged the view that the urban landscape is inferior to the rural, but the towns and cities are where most people live and the young must explore what is to hand, finding adventure, stimulus, and even beauty in those things which are considered ugly by conventional standards. The trades unionist Jack Jones, former General Secretary of the Transport and General Workers' Union, and still an active campaigner for pensioners, was born in York Street, Garston, in 1913, 'a long street of poor and mean terraced houses'. In his autobiography, *Union Man* (1986), Jones describes his childhood in the dockside streets: 'We walked past the copper works, the tannery, Grayson's shipyard, the bobbin works (making bobbins for the textile industry), a derelict glass works and King's ship-breaking yard, and there we were on shore, a wonderful if muddy playground when we tired of playing our games in the street.' On another occasion he would wander into the local shipyard 'to wonder at everything around me: the noise of riveting, hammering; the fumes and the flashes; the movement of the cranes; the red-hot rivets...'

Jack Jones's first job was as an apprentice with a firm making components for the shipbuilding industry. It had no canteen so he was in the habit of taking his sandwiches to the Cocoa Rooms on the Dock Road: 'There I would buy a mug of strong tea, or occasionally a mug of soup. Its attractions didn't end there, for it became a debating centre.' The Cocoa Rooms, or 'cokes', were originally introduced by the temperance campaigners to wean the working classes off drink and one of their specialities was a slab of fruit cake called a 'wet nellie'. My Auntie Nellie (in Liverpool, by the way, the correct pronunciation of 'auntie' is 'anti', as in 'anti-nuclear device'), for understandable reasons, always insisted that the correct term was 'wet neller'.

There was much for a budding political activist to talk about in the cokes, for life in the early decades of the twentieth century was still tough in Liverpool, the grim nineteenth century still casting its shadow, the courts and cellars, the poverty and slums, the barefoot children, still ubiquitous. Life on the docks was made tougher by the casual system of hiring, a system which was not abolished until 1972, with dockers mustering each morning before the foreman, never knowing whether they would get a job or not. If there is a certain recklessness – or fecklessness if you will – in the Liverpool character when it comes to surviving day to day, then this system, and that of the similarly casually hired seaman, must have a part in the explanation. As Jones explains, it was not an easy way to live:

> Standing about waiting for work in the early morning near the river was bad enough, then to be subjected to the 'you, you, and you!' calls of the foreman stretched tolerance to the limit, but it had to be accepted because of the urgent need for work. Many of the men with me had wives and children and their misery when they couldn't get a job was heart-rending... I can see in my mind's eye now the grey, drawn faces of the men who were turned away.

As a child I was once taken aside by an odd job man called Joe Joyce who explained to me – he must have thought that the knowledge would do me good – how, as a young man on the docks, he had been in those morning crowds, begging for work. He had been enraged by the way some of the men jumped on the backs of the men in front in order to secure the foreman's eye. He felt this was an abandonment of dignity on their part. His eyes had wandered now back to that scene as he declared defiantly, still angry all these years later at the men's behaviour: 'I'm as 'umble as a beggar; burr'ave got me dignity.'

Dockers also worked on piece rates, another kind of provisional existence which had its human costs: 'Because it was piecework, men worked fast and sometimes dangerously,' wrote Jack Jones. 'Accidents occurred, partly because of this but mainly because safety arrangements were inadequate.'

Another act of working-class defiance took place in that first decade of the twentieth century, on 27th June 1904, three weeks before King Edward VII came to Liverpool to lay the foundation stone for the Liverpool cathedral on 19th July, surrounded by seven thousand invited guests on St James's Mount. One of the stonemasons, who claimed to have cut the first stone on the cathedral site (he would eventually die in 1933 of silicosis, the stone mason's disease), was Fred Bower. With his fellow socialist, the docker James Larkin, he placed an envelope of tin containing a message to the future in the foundations of the cathedral, three weeks before the King arrived. The two men came from opposite sides of Liverpool's religious divide and took part, on Orangeman's Day 1912, in a symbolic march with banners of orange and green intertwined, organised by another union leader, Tom Mann, seeking to replace religious sectarianism with socialist solidarity. Bower and Larkin placed in the receptacle a copy each of the leftist newspapers *The Clarion* and the *Labour Leader* together with a note to posterity:

To the Finders, Hail!

We, the wage slaves employed on the erection of this cathedral, to be dedicated to the worship of the unemployed Jewish carpenter, hail ye! Within a stone's throw from here, human beings are housed in slums not fit for swine. This message, written on trust-produced paper with trust-produced inks, is to tell ye how we today are at the mercy of trusts. Building fabrics, clothing, fuel, transport, are all in the hands of money-mad, soul-destroying trusts. We can sell only our labour power, as wage slaves, on their terms. The money trusts today own us. In your own day, you will, thanks to the efforts of past and present agitators for economic freedom, own the trusts. Yours will indeed, compared to ours of today, be a happier existence. See to it, therefore, that ye, too, work for the betterment of *all*, and so justify your existence by leaving the world the better for your having lived in it. Thus and thus only shall come about the Kingdom of 'God' or 'Good' on Earth. Hail, Comrades, and Farewell.

Yours sincerely,

'A Wage Slave'.

This message, of which very few people in Liverpool are aware (Bower revealed it twenty years later in his autobiography, *Rolling Stonemason* (1936)), was put between compressed sheets of tin and placed between two courses of brick in the foundations of the cathedral.

At around this time, in the wake of the 1908 Children Act, James Samuelson published the study mentioned earlier, *The Children of Our Slums* (1911), which confirmed by observation of Liverpool the facts of persistent urban poverty. It was hardly surprising that movements of resistance and change

144

began to stir. The Liverpool Transport Strike of 1911 was a major landmark.

What made this strike unique was that it relied for its success on solidarity between various unions instead of action being confined, as hitherto, within individual trades. First the seamen struck for ten shillings more than the then standard wage of £4.10s. Throughout the summer of 1911, for 72 days, virtually all transport workers in the port were on strike at one time or another, and their action was taking place in a context of national industrial action. In June a national seamen's stike was called and in August there was a national railway strike, as well as a rash of individual strikes across Britain by various groups of workers. Winston Churchill compared the situation to a civil war and answered the call of Liverpool magistrates for extra police. These were drafted in from Leeds and Birmingham. Troops were also stationed around the city. 'If troops are not sufficient,' Churchill told the Lord Mayor, 'you should ask for more.' The build-up of police and troops reached its peak on Sunday 13th August, the day when the Strike Committee planned a demonstration at St George's Plateau. This day would come to be known as Bloody Sunday.

An estimated 60,000 workers filled the plateau to listen to Tom Mann, chairman of the Strike Committee, who defied Churchill to do his worst. After a small disturbance the authorities decided to instruct police to clear the area and a magistrate took Mann's place on the platform to read the Riot Act. Before people could disperse peacefully mounted police charged in with long wooden truncheons. Fifteen-year-old George Garrett was in the crowd and sustained a broken nose and several smashed teeth from a full blow in the face from one of the truncheons. 'This is another thing I will never forget,' wrote Bessie Braddock, another twelve-year-old witness receiving a political education that day, 'the charge of well-fed police on superb horses, the batons swinging, enough half-starved workers falling to fill every hospital in Liverpool.' Braddock had been present at an earlier demonstration in the same place in the harsh winter of 1906 at a gathering of the unemployed when she was seven: 'I remember the faces of the unemployed when the soup ran out. I remember their dull eyes and their thin, blue lips. I remember blank, hopeless stares, day after day, week after week, all through the hard winter of 1906–7.'

Most economic historians agree that the very early years of the twentieth century mark the apogee of Liverpool's commercial success as a port, yet little of that wealth was trickling down to these men and their families. Braddock pointed out that St George's Plateau was surrounded by the commercial magnificence of Liverpool: 'But that winter the workers queued here for farthing bowls of soup served with hunks of bread. Their faces, white with malnutrition and cold, stood out tiny and perishable against the black, enduring stone buildings… Of the city's seven hundred thousand people a thousand were dying of starvation and tens of thousands, men, women, and children, were hungry, cold and sick.' The soup was served up by the *Clarion* van, a mobile caravan associated with that socialist newspaper (read avidly by my grandfather in his Bootle barber's shop) and the soup was made by local volunteers including Braddock's mother, Mary Bamber, the political activist. On the side of the *Clarion* van were painted the slogans 'Without the Workers We Cannot Win' and 'SOCIALISM, a system of Government that will make poverty impossible'. Braddock later wrote: 'It was the unemployed workers of Liverpool in 1906–7 who made me a rebel… suffering in Liverpool came more quickly and was more general than in most other cities.' After the strike union membership soared. 31,000 dockers, for example were unionised in November 1911 when there had only been 8,000 in May.

This great surge of political radicalism came to an end only because of the outbreak of the Great War. But the conditions that bred it remained for the future.

14

The Infantry Officer

In May 1915 the poet Siegfried Sassoon reported to the 3rd Battalion of the Royal Welch Fusiliers at its Wartime Training Depot at what he would call 'the dingy suburb of Litherland' in north Liverpool. The Depot was situated between Brotherton's Ammunition Factory and a large Roman Catholic cemetery. These sights, his biographer Jean Moorcroft Wilson points out, taken with 'the smoking chimneys of Bryant and May's match factory half a mile away, could not have been a cheering sight'. To escape this rather dreary spot (Litherland always make me think of the sausage factory which I used to pass on the bus, a fat porker with a sausage on a fork over his shoulder fixed to the façade) Sassoon would take a walk down to the shore at Seaforth or catch the train to Formby to play golf. In his *Memoirs of an Infantry Officer* (1930), Sassoon gives his own thumbnail sketch of the Depot: 'Factory-hooters and ships' foghorns out on the Mersey sometimes combined in huge unhappy dissonances; their sound seemed one with the smoke-drifted munition works, the rubble of industrial suburbs, and the canal that crawled squalidly out into blighted and forbidding farmlands which were only waiting to be built over.'

But Sassoon had other things on his mind in 1915. His opposition to the war was growing to a crisis which must have coloured his reaction to Liverpool. Moreover, he seems to have had a great deal of time on his hands to brood. At least once a week he took the electric train to Formby, a twenty-minute ride, where the golf club was 'famous for its bracing air, comfortable Club House, and superlatively good war-time food'. Usually he played alone, and often had the entire links to himself, 'which was no disadvantage, since I have always been addicted to my own company'. The other diversion was going into the centre of Liverpool to what he calls in the book the Olympic Hotel but which is obviously the Adelphi: 'Never having crossed the Atlantic, I did not realize that the Hotel was an American importation, but I know that the whole thing might have been brought over from New York in the mind of a first-class passenger... Everything was white and gilt and smooth; it was, so to speak, an air-tight Paradise made of imitation marble.'

After Sassoon had delivered his statement against the war to his superiors he again took the train to Formby. It was a Saturday afternoon and this time there was to be no golf:

> Wandering along the sand dunes I felt outlawed, bitter, and baited. I wanted something to smash and trample on, and in a paroxysm of exasperation I performed the time-honoured gesture of shaking my clenched fists at the sky. Feeling no better for that, I ripped the MC ribbon off my tunic and threw it into the mouth of the Mersey. Weighted with significance, as this action was, it would have felt more conclusive had the ribbon been heavier. As it was, the poor little thing fell weakly on to the water and floated away as though aware of its own futility... Watching a big boat which was steaming along the horizon, I realized that

protesting against the prolongation of the War was about as much use as shouting at the people on board that ship.

The next day Sassoon returned to the beach at Formby (where I used to swim as a child, in spite of the driftwood, rubbish and occasional deposits of oil) in the company of a friend, David Cromlech. The latter told Sassoon that he would not be court-martialled but declared insane and put in an asylum for the rest of the war. The poet saw no alternative but to agree to this proposal: 'As soon as the words were out of my mouth I sat down on an old wooden breakwater. So that was the end of my grand gesture. I ought to have known that the blighters would do me down somehow, I thought, scowling heavily at the sea.'

'To depart and arrive are beautiful,' observed the Czech writer Karel Čapek, who arrived in Liverpool six years after the end of the war. He found the Anglican cathedral, on which work had begun twenty years earlier in 1904, 'as large and hopeless as the ruins of the baths of Caracalla in Rome', but in spite of a 'wretched inn' with a bed 'smelling like a cask of cabbage' he was enchanted by the life of the port:

> yellow water, bellowing steam ferries, tugboats, pot-bellied, black sows rocking on the waves, white, transatlantic liners, docks, basins, towers, cranes, silos, elevators, smoking factories, stevedores, skiffs, warehouses, shipyards, barrels, chests, parcels, chimneys, masts, rigging, trains, smoke, chaos, hooting, ringing, hammering, puffing, the ruptured bellies of ships, the stench of horses, of sweat, urine and waste from all continents of the world.

'If I heaped up words for another half an hour, I wouldn't achieve the full number, confusion, and expanse which is called Liverpool,' concluded Čapek in his *Letters from England* (1924).

Another writer more interested in departure than arrival was Malcolm Lowry, author of one of the great twentieth-century novels, *Under the Volcano*. If we are to be pedantic, he was not a Liverpudlian but was born in Liscard on the Wirral, the family moving to Caldy in 1912. But his father, Arthur Osborne Lowry, was a successful Liverpool cotton broker who had himself been born in Admiral Street, Toxteth. Lowry's mother was also a Liverpudlian, daughter of a master mariner and born in Handel Street in the same district. Every day, Lowry senior would catch the ferry across the Mersey to the cotton exchange, but there was little chance of his son following in his father's footsteps. Steeped in the literature of the sea – Eugene O'Neill's early sea plays and Jack London's *The Sea Wolf* – Lowry longed to go to sea. In one of his stories he wrote that in Liverpool – 'that terrible city whose main street is the ocean' – there was 'an enormous sense of sea and ships' to which a young boy could not be indifferent, and there grew in him what he called in *Ultramarine*, his first novel, 'an inborn craving for the unrest of the sea'. Quite early in his life these romantic notions were put to the rough test of reality when he shipped on a Blue Funnel boat for the Far East, the SS *Pyrrhus*, in his year between public school and Cambridge. Before this, as an adolescent, he had been morbidly fascinated by the Anatomy Museum in Paradise Street 'which had a section designed to warn unwary seamen against the dire consequences of venereal disease'. Situated in the city's red light district, the museum's 'pickled testicles' were regularly inspected by the young Lowry.

On 14th May 1927 Lowry sailed on the *Pyrrhus* as a deck-boy. His departure turned into an event, with reporters from the *Liverpool Echo* on hand to record the scene. 'RICH BOY AS DECK HAND' was the eventual headline. To compound Lowry's shame (and probable apprehension about the brewing reaction of the crew to the posh greenhorn) his father arranged to have him driven to the ship in the family Rolls Royce. Lowry bravely talked himself up to the reporter: 'No silk-cushion youth for me, I want to see the world, and rub shoulders with its oddities, and get some experience of life before I go back to Cambridge University.' The novel *Ultramarine* would later reflect the reality of the subsequent voyage. Mrs Lowry then weighed in with the observation: 'He is bent on a literary career, and his short-story writing is all to him. Of course, he has taken his ukulele with him, and he hopes to compose some more Charlestons during the voyage.' Fortunately for Lowry, by the time the *Echo* appeared he was far out in the Irish Sea, where there would be quite enough shoulder-rubbing with the 'oddities' amongst the crew without this extra provocation to their sarcasm.

While the Lowry chauffeur-driven Rolls purred through the dock gates, elsewhere in Liverpool, another scene met the eye in the 1920s and 1930s. 'The streets swarmed with shoeless children,' Bessie Braddock recalled, 'whose feet were washed and anointed at free foot clinics on Sunday mornings. A child in boots could collect a crowd of bootless children.' In case this seems implausible or tendentious there is evidence in a remarkable collection of photographs in Liverpool's City Engineer's Department which it started to commission in 1897, a selection of which were published in 1993 by Colin Wilkinson as *The Streets of Liverpool* (the title alluding to an earlier work of that name by James Stonehouse published in 1869). These photographs of the city and its inhabitants are fascinating but one frame clearly shows a group of shoeless street children. It is dated 1926.

Bessie Braddock – later a scourge of the Bevanite Left – began as a firebrand, born in Zante Street in 1899, the daughter of Mary Bamber, who had been dubbed by Sylvia Pankhurst 'the finest fighting platform speaker in the country'. When she became an MP in 1945, the *Daily Express* observed:

> Mrs Braddock, the member for the Exchange Division of Liverpool can fairly be described as a character among the Labour women. Very forthright in her speech, strong in her Labour faith, she is inclined to express her views of her opponents with a certain contemptuous freedom, and she never hesitates to call a spade a spade. Watching her it is easy to see that she finds listening to a provocative opponent something of a strain. There is nothing frail about her; indeed her deportment gives the impression of great vigour.

She was a large lady in every sense. She once told the assembled members of the Liverpool Cotton Association: 'I am more concerned about the workhouse not being re-opened than I am about the Cotton Exchange.' She was impatient with the 'artificiality' of London and its easy assumption of privilege: 'There is too much wealth floating around there,' she said during the 1950 election campaign. 'When I feel I am getting too complacent I walk around some of the poorer streets of Liverpool and that wakes me up.'

Bessie Braddock's career as a politician, fuelled by those childhood experiences of witnessing the unemployed and the hungry, began locally when she stood for St Anne's ward for the City Council in 1930. Just 75 years ago this is what she saw:

> It was a frightful place. The houses were shocking and the cellars worse. If you ignored the front doors, flanked by overflowing dustbins, and went down the steps beside them, you found hundreds of families living where perpetually-burning candles or oil lamps fought the gloom. Many cellars had water grids, and in stormy weather the water rose into them from the sewers. They were always damp of course.

153

The houses were enormous, abandoned by the rich cotton and shipping bosses who built them but who had now moved out to more salubrious places in the suburbs. They had first been occupied by the Irish labourers who came over at the time of the potato famine. Sometimes there were as many as twenty rooms in one house, each one containing a family. A typical room contained a double bed, divided so that six children could sleep on the mattress – three at one end, three at the other. When the parents came home they climbed over the children to the base of the bed, which they shared with the youngest ones:

> Rest was fitful, for they had to listen for the 'nightman' employed by Liverpool Corporation to go round after midnight, burst into the rooms and count the occupants. The poor conspired to escape prosecution on overcrowding and morals charges by passing news of his approach with special knocks on the walls and ceilings of the houses. At this alarm, dozens of sleepy kids would scramble from their beds and decamp into dark back-alleys to hide until he went away.

This reads like a nightmarish parody of the worst kind of social policy, where the victims are transformed into perpetrators, and public intervention attacks with vigour the symptoms not the disease.

'Mind, Bessie,' the tenants would say when she came to do her rounds, fearful that she would catch from them some disease.

People fought back, of course, and there was much union militancy in the 1920s and 1930s, which also saw the foundation of socialist cultural institutions such as the Merseyside Unity Theatre in Mount Pleasant. After the Second World War, the Labour MP Eric Heffer was its chairman and the Unity

154

Theatre was part of a national movement with 250 groups. In 1922, the first national hunger march had taken place and there is a fine description of it by George Garrett. One of his best pieces of reportage – explaining why he was so admired by Orwell – was *Liverpool 1921–22*. Garrett says of this period: 'In Liverpool with its sixty thousand out-of-works, mass disillusionment, degradation and raggedness were pronounced. But resentment only seethed in small groups around the Labour Exchanges, or was muttered on back-street corners, or screamed inside slum hovels. It had yet to be joined.' Liverpool Poor Law officials who gave out pitifully small amounts of parish outdoor relief admitted that distress in the city was worse in 1921 than at any period since 1907. It was a time when the Workhouse Guardians of Poplar in East London had gone to prison for giving higher scales of relief and there was pressure for the system of workhouse tickets for bread, tea, soap and so on to be replaced by cash outdoor relief. A meeting was called in Liverpool in September 1921 to demand this. What made it special was that it was held on the Exchange Flags, where normally no working men were seen, the Flags being the preserve of men like Arthur O. Lowry. In Garrett's words,

> The Exchange Flags, a closed-in quad with its venerable-looking buildings, had always been forbidden ground to the city's working men. Here the well-dressed merchants and brokers met daily in the centre around a squat Trafalgar memorial to transact their business deals. The wide-domed Town Hall backed on to one side, its high windows uncurtained, while those of the buildings opposite bore the gilded names of century-old firms. Arched passage-ways served as short-cuts to the busy streets roundabout, but were never used by workmen except by those with a repair-job on the Flags.

155

This was not, however, the first time that the Flags had seen an outbreak of popular protest. In the summer of 1775, largely as a result of the American War of Independence, around half of Liverpool's seamen were unemployed. Sensing their advantage, the employers reduced the pay for rigging out a ship for a voyage from 30 to 20 shillings. Outraged sailors who had just rigged out the *Derby* and who had found themselves offered 20*s* returned to the ship and cut down the rigging. The same treatment was quickly meted out to the rest of the rigged ships in the port. When magistrates arrested and imprisoned nine men the prison was surrounded by two to three thousand seamen who managed to secure the release of the men. They then marched to the town hall behind a red flag and assembled on the Flags. On the fifth day of the protest the mayor agreed to meet a delegation of sailors and it seemed that the merchants had agreed to restore the original rates. But they then hired a body of armed men, some of whom were installed inside the town hall and who fired on the unarmed strikers on the Flags. Possibly as many as seven strikers were killed and more than ten injured. In a fury the seamen went aboard the ships to collect cannon which were drawn up around the town hall. The next day, with red ribbons in their hats, and a red flag raised high, they began to bombard the town hall, killing four more people. The authorities called out the cavalry who hunted down and arrested up to 60 sailors and marched them off to Lancaster gaol. Only twelve, however, were finally indicted. Eight were found guilty but all were discharged on agreeing to enlist in the Navy – itself probably punishment enough in the eighteenth century.

In September 1921 the principal speaker was a policeman, a veteran of the 1911 police strike, but a policeman nevertheless and therefore suspect in the eyes of some of the men. Ten thousand men crowded into the Flags and demanded that a deputation be seen by the Lord Mayor who, seeing the crowd, agreed, showing himself afterwards on the balcony of the Town Hall like the Pontiff. In the wake of this demonstration an organising committee was established and a series of 'nuisance marches' was organised in which thousands of unemployed men would gather in a street such as Lord Street, peacefully, arms linked, bringing traffic to a halt. They had pinned their yellow unemployment cards to their lapels. 'Most of the men wore war medals too,' Garrett noted, adding, 'or pawn-tickets to prove they had recently possessed them.'

Another demonstration followed, this time on St George's Plateau, and there were calls by some for another nuisance march. Instead the leaders proposed that there should be a mass peaceful invasion of the Walker Art Gallery. 'We'll all be art critics this afternoon,' declared the former police-striker. 'Those places are as much for us as anybody else. They belong to the public.' Then the authorities panicked and hundreds of foot-police appeared, laying about them with truncheons. Mounted police charged the crowd. 'Unlike the half-nourished unemployed they were privileged to carry truncheons and sticks and were cracking everybody they could lay hand on,' wrote Garrett. Those trapped inside the Gallery were the most badly beaten. Four committee members were later rounded up by detectives and thrown into a cell. The following week, after a remand hearing, all the cases came to court and many of the 160 defendants, their heads bandaged, were dealt with quickly by fines or by being bound over. They were lucky that the elderly magistrate was 'extremely tolerant' and struck them as fair, especially in the face of what they saw as erroneous and hostile evidence from the police witnesses. On one day of the trial a defendant was late because '[there] was no clock. We had to pawn it last night for something to eat.' The magistrate led the court in laughter. The remaining prisoners were released on heavy bail and committed to the Sessions.

When the trial opened at the Sessions an attempt was made to link the demonstrators to Moscow and a prosecuting counsel asked one seaman: 'Do you receive any money from a certain government?' When the man said yes, counsel couldn't believe his luck and gleefully pressed home his advantage: 'What is the name of that government?' The reply came: 'The British Government. I'm on the dole.'

The Recorder sentenced the men to one day's imprisonment which meant that they were immediately released. He later expressed deep concern about the 'profoundly disquieting' behaviour of the police. 'There is nothing in the police evidence to suggest that there should be any violence,' he said. 'I think most unnecessary force was used to these men in the Walker Art Gallery.' He said that one reason he had not sent the defendants to prison was because they had already been 'improperly punished' by the police.

The nuisance marches continued but the Liverpool Poor Law Guardians stubbornly refused to follow the example of neighbouring towns and grant the new relief scales. The terrible memory of the workhouse among the Liverpool poor was behind the call for an end to the pre-war attitude to unemployment. Their demand was now 'Work or Maintenance'. No more charity soup-lines. Eventually, after more demonstrations, the Guardians gave in and the new scales were applied. But the hunger marches went on.

Ten years later, in September 1932, the unemployed were on the streets again. 34 per cent of men in the 18–64 age group were now jobless. According to the Liverpool historian Harold Hikins, '[in] the last two weeks of September 1932, Birkenhead and Liverpool were in a state of near insurrection'. Demonstrations, battles with the police, and looting of shops went on in Birkenhead for four days from 19th September.

The *casus belli* was the means test. The National Unemployed Workers' Movement organised a march to the home of the much hated Tory Chairman of the Public Assistance Committee, Alderman Baker. Clashes with police ensued and the protestors responded by laying siege to a police station, penning the officers inside. On one demonstration the bloodstained shirt of a man called Paddy Davin was held aloft on a pole. He had died from a fall after a police rooftop chase. When Bob Lovell, an official of the International Class War Prisoners' Aid Society, arrived from London to arrange the defence of some of the arrested men he asked one of them, Bill McBeth, who had chosen to defend himself, what his defence would be. 'There's only one line of defence I can take,' replied McBeth, 'I didn't throw enough stones.' Lovell warned that this would mean his being sent down for ever. 'What's the difference?' McBeth retorted. 'They'll have to keep me, and I can't afford to live on the dole.' He was eventually sentenced to nine months' hard labour.

In 1933 J. B. Priestley arrived in Liverpool on his *English Journey*. He admitted that he always arrived in Liverpool in inauspicious weather and was consequently always unfair to it. This time he found that '[the] centre is imposing, dignified and darkish, like a city in a rather gloomy Victorian novel'. The Mersey itself was 'a misty nothingness hooting dismally'. But it was the Irish that finished the city for him. He exulted at the thought of what a 'grand clearance' of them would do for Liverpool: 'what a fine exit of ignorance and dirt and drunkenness and disease'. His sensitive analysis was that '[these] Irish flocked over here to be navvies and dock hands and casual labourers... they have settled in the nearest poor quarter and turned it into a slum, or, finding a slum, have promptly settled down to out-slum it... I imagine Liverpool would be glad to be rid of them now.'

A less bigoted observer, three years later, was George Orwell, who arrived on 25th February 1936 and met Garrett. He was 'greatly impressed' by him and was aware of his writing for the *Adelphi* magazine under the pseudonym Matt Low:

> He is a biggish hefty chap of about 36, Liverpool-Irish, brought up a Catholic but now a Communist. He says he has had about 9 months' work in (I think) about the last 6 years. He went to sea as a lad and was at sea about ten years, then worked as a docker. During the war he was torpedoed on a ship that sank in 7 minutes, but they had expected to be torpedoed and had got their boats ready, and were all saved except the wireless operator, who refused to leave his post until he had got an answer. He also worked in an illicit brewery in Chicago during Prohibition, saw various hold-ups, saw Battling Ski immediately after he had been shot in a street brawl etc etc.

All this makes one wish that Garrett had had time to write more of that 'etc etc', but he told Orwell that living in two rooms on the dole with a wife and several children made it impossible to settle to any long work. Short stories were all he could manage. In addition, '[apart] from the enormous unemployment in Liverpool it is almost impossible for him to get work because he is blacklisted everywhere as a Communist'.

Garrett took Orwell down to the docks to see the hiring system for himself. When they arrived there were about 200 men waiting in a ring, held back by the police. A fruit ship was unloading and the tussle to get hired had resulted in a fight and the calling out of the police. The foreman came out of a shed looking for another ten men in addition to the gangs he had hired earlier in the day. He walked around picking out a man here and there. 'He would pause,' Orwell observed, 'select a man, take him by the shoulder and haul him forward, exactly as at a sale of cattle. Presently he announced that was all. A sort of groan went up from the remaining dockers, and they trailed off, about 50 men having been engaged out of 200.' These unemployed casual dockers were required to sign on twice a day, otherwise they were presumed to have been working and their dole docked for the day.

Although, like most observers, Orwell was appalled by the casual hiring system shown to him by Garrett, he was impressed by the Corporation's attempts in 1936 to build working-class housing, particularly the large deck-access flats in the middle of the city 'imitated from those in Vienna'. He noted a paradox that the Tory Corporation (Liverpool has never been, notwithstanding its bolshie reputation, a Red city for other than sporadic episodes) was 'entirely ruthless towards private ownership', pulling down slums without compensation. Its use of public funds to rehouse the poor was 'in effect a Socialist measure'. While in the city Orwell went through the Mersey tunnel to see the model workers' housing at Port Sunlight where the soap manufacturer Lord Leverhulme had built accommodation for his company's staff. Before leaving Liverpool Orwell bought a couple of brass candlesticks and a ship in a bottle for nine shillings.

George Garrett thought the Old Etonian had been had.

15

Faces Without Laughter

Just before the outbreak of the Second World War the Greek writer Nikos Kazantzakis, author of *Zorba the Greek*, arrived in Liverpool on a journey through England. He was not the first Greek writer to be associated with the city for, nearly a century earlier, the family of one of the greatest modern Greek poets, Constantine Cavafy, settled for three years in Liverpool. The poet's father, Peter John Cavafy, managed the family trading firm Cassavetti, Cavafy & Co., importing mostly wheat and cotton from Egypt, and from 1852 he lived at 33 Bedford Street South. Much later, after her husband's death in 1873, Haricleia Cavafy and her three children, including the future poet, Constantine, who had been born in Alexandria, returned to Liverpool to live at 12 Balmoral Road. The children would have been educated locally but Cavafy left no record of his sojourn in the city. When the firm crashed in 1876 the family moved to less grand lodgings in Huskisson Street until they were ready to return to Alexandria. Liverpool retains a Greek community and 'the kebab house', as it was simply known to students like myself in the 1970s, has been joined by many other Greek restaurants, the most visible sign for others of the continuing presence of the Liverpool Greeks. The existence of a Greek community in a large seaport is not at all surprising but Liverpool's has still to find its historian.

Kazantzakis falls into the disenchanted category of foreign observer of Liverpool. He found it, in August 1939, 'a still more hideous city' than Birmingham which he had just left. He paid grudging tribute to the great warehouses and quays but retained a view that the 'big, antipathetic city' was mere 'modern organised ugliness' – his account appears in a section of his *England: A Travel Journal* (1965) headed 'Grime-Stained Cities' – lacking, in spite of all those neo-classical buildings, any true trace of the 'immortal Greek harmony'. What repelled him most of all was the fact that 'the endless uniform rows of smoke-stained brick houses present an unbearable spectacle, as do the streets bereft of charm and the faces without laughter'. As in Birmingham 'terror overcomes you when you see the people scurrying like ants', and the frantic activity in the Exchange. The only redeeming feature of this 'graceless city' was a meeting with a fellow Greek, Peter Vlastos, who lived 'alongside a park dense with foliage and far removed from noise and smoke, in a noble house surrounded by tall trees'. Shutting out the awfulness of Liverpool he spent the remainder of his time with this 'great lover and master of the word'. Peter Vlastos lived in Fulwood Park in what Kazantzakis told a Greek friend was 'a manor house' which was clearly a refuge for the writer. He left the next day 'as though someone were chasing me'.

Kazantzakis' reference to the 'faces without laughter' echoes an observation I made earlier about a certain feature of Liverpool humour, call it deadpan, which is the opposite of chuckling jollity and which can deceive. Many of the characters in Phil Redmond's popular serial (controversially axed by

Channel 4) *Brookside* exhibited this in ways that some Liverpudlians, who did not wish to see this reflected back at them, did not like. *Brookside* had its ardent fans, and it was innovative in its genre, but I was one of those who found a certain grimness in it, one that could have been lightened, I felt, by a dash of the more joshing kind of Liverpool humour.

After the Second World War Liverpool was slow to clear its slums and it retained some of those ugly features noticed by Kazantzakis. 'No great city outside England, and few inside,' wrote John Willett in his *Art in a City*, one of the more interesting and perceptive modern books about Liverpool, 'have been so slow to set themselves straight after the war, and for a long while the effect on the citizens was, to say the least of it, disheartening'. But he also noted 'a largeness of spirit here which contrasts unexpectedly with the various symptoms of decline'. Another way of putting this might be that Liverpool deserved better, that its people have, too often, been let down. And too often it is they who have been blamed, rather than those in whose power it was to make a better shot. John Willett, whose ostensible purpose was to make a general survey of the visual arts in Liverpool but who achieved rather more than this, noted another feature of Liverpool, its way of making friends. 'It is difficult to have much to do with Liverpool without developing a special affection for the place. A special affection, because it also embraces exasperation and regret at the conditions in which many of its inhabitants have had to live'.

But the official version of the 1960s was that Liverpool was at the epicentre of a revolution in popular culture. It was swinging. It was the home of the Beatles – about whom I have had virtually nothing to say in this book because so much has already been said. As a schoolboy, wrestling with some far from swinging realities, I was astonished to read, around the middle of that decade of supposed liberation, a quotation by the American beat poet, Allen Ginsberg: 'Liverpool...is at the present moment the centre of consciousness of the human universe. They're resurrecting the human form divine there – all those beautiful youths with long, golden archangelic hair.'

I recall showing this astonishing claim (which had been repeated on the cover of the Liverpool University student magazine, *Sphinx*) to my best friend, Phil, who had won a scholarship to read English at Oxford, where the dons at St Catherine's College were delighted by this *echt*-Scouse verbal artist's vivid and madly inventive expressions. Phil took the magazine from me, brushed back his 'long golden archangelic hair', stared for a minute at the cover, and observed acidly: 'Arsehole of the universe, Niggsie.'

The Beatles were formed in 1960. They started recording for EMI in 1962 when I was ten years old. A rash of Liverpool TV playwrights such as Alun Owen – when original drama of that kind was still flourishing on Britain's television networks – also came to prominence in the 1960s. And there were the Liverpool poets. John Willett comments:

> Under the ballyhoo and the apparent banalities [and weren't there plenty of those!] it was a fresh wave of young Liverpudlians, bright products of the post-war state school system, who had found their own way of expressing themselves without any noticeable advice or encouragement from anybody else. With their special brand of anarchy, aggressive yet human, they were just one jump ahead of their contemporaries in other British cities, and there is no reason why their energies should not have found other channels.

There was an interesting continuum in Liverpool from the pop music culture to the more avant-garde art fields, exemplified by the career of the 'fifth Beatle', Stuart Sutcliffe. He had been a friend of John Lennon at Liverpool College of Art and after a 1960 Hamburg tour he stayed behind to study at the State High School for Art. When he died of a brain tumour at Hamburg in 1962 aged 21 he was, in Willett's view, 'an outstanding loss to Liverpool and quite possibly to English painting'.

The Beatles tended to gloss over their lower-middle-class origins but in the case of an artist such as Arthur Dooley, the sculptor, his working-class credentials gleamed brightly. When I was a child Dooley, the Catholic-Communist, was a regular on the local news channels, always ready with a defiant and quotable view on a range of topics. He was famous for riding a white horse through the centre of Liverpool in protest at the gusto with which the authorities were destroying historic buildings in the city. The son of a Liverpool docker, he had spent nine years in the Irish Guards and had worked at the Dunlop tyre factory at Speke before setting himself up as a self-taught sculptor at the beginning of the 1960s. Outside his studio in Seel Street was the sign A DOOLEY SCULPTOR. His bronze figures were always striking and interesting and he received the commission to work the Stations of the Cross for a new Catholic church at Leyland in Lancashire. He approached the architect of the church and asked if he could get an advance of £400. Appalled at this breach of professional decorum, the architect said that dipping into his back pocket for a sub was out of the question. This was not, for goodness' sake, a building-site. 'All right then; give us five pounds,' replied Dooley, unabashed.

On one occasion an interview with the BBC *Tonight* programme couldn't be broadcast owing to the sculptor's language. His views on the art schools attended by Lennon and McCartney were equally vigorous: 'Three thousand a year and as much crumpet as you can eat,' was his characterisation

166

of the life of the art school lecturer. He was cynical about the intimate connection between art and the art of self-promotion but was no slouch himself in exploiting opportunities for publicity. But he was also a genuine artist. Willett met him in the mid-1960s and found him '[a] big, dirty, sad-looking chap humped over a tiny coffee table' and showing 'utter contempt for the College, for the Walker Art Gallery, for pretty well everything'.

The Liverpool Playhouse in the mid-sixties was also feeling the excitement of the times, as my friend Colin Lovelace, then assistant manager of the theatre, explains:

> The plays of Behan, Osborne, Arthur Miller and Brecht, put on by David Scase at the Playhouse in the mid-Sixties with actors like Steven Berkoff, Patrick Stewart, Anthony Hopkins and Jean Boht, reflected Scase's left wing politics and his long apprenticeship with Joan Littlewood. The programme was a complete break from the staid programme of the Fifties but it exactly suited and reflected contemporary Liverpool, attracting a new, younger, less stuffy audience which had been put off in the past by polite drawing room comedies and musical revues served in evening dress.

Lovelace continues:

> The Beatles had made Liverpool fashionable and in 1964 Harold Wilson, as Prime Minister and MP for Huyton had made it politically interesting. I remember running through the centre of Liverpool with a huge crowd, on election night, 1964 on my way to the Election Party at the Adelphi amidst an atmosphere vibrant and electric with expectation that a new era was dawning after thirteen years of Conservative government.'

And in the middle of all this excitement, work was beginning on the reconstruction of the city centre with the erection of the St John's Tower right next door to the Playhouse in Williamson Square. The message put out by the developers and the City Council to justify the tearing down of so many 'dilapidated' buildings was 'renewal', and working in the theatre in Liverpool at the time, we saw ourselves in the vanguard of all this change.

Added to this heady brew, the old Hope Hall cinema, with its seemingly permanent showing of *The Song of Bernadette*, was replaced by the Everyman Theatre. A rival to the Playhouse, yes, and not always a very friendly one, but a theatre with an even more adventurous artistic policy and a galaxy of future stars such as Jonathan Pryce and Alison Steadman, directed by the future boss of the RSC, Terry Hands.

To be young and involved in all this going on in Liverpool was for me to be in heaven and I remember Jenny Smith, one of the assistant stage managers, saying to me at a party in my flat in Canning Street: 'This time, 1965. It's really special here isn't it ? We'll never forget it.' And we haven't.

The Liverpool poets who also sprang on to the scene in the 1960s were altogether smoother operators than rough diamonds like Dooley, ably taken up by metropolitan critics and reputation-makers, and achieving success with publications such as the best-selling Penguin anthology *The Mersey Sound*, issued in 1967. The cover of the first edition was a collage of Beatles and Liverpool images and the three poets represented – Adrian Henri, Roger McGough and Brian Patten – rode the wave of media interest in Liverpool in the sixties. The Liverpool poets were entertainers, often combining poetry and music – McGough was a member of a group called The Scaffold – and the reading was central to their careers. As a teenager at the time, discovering poetry, and trying for the first time to write it, I was in two minds about all this. There was a certain glamour in their presence in bars like the Philharmonic Hotel where under-age *literati* could rub shoulders with them, but I wondered how good this stuff really was.

One morning my professor at Liverpool University, Kenneth Allott, a fine poet of 1930s' vintage and an intelligent anthologist, came in with a copy of Philip Larkin's new *Oxford Book of Twentieth Century Verse* and expressed disgust at the inclusion of some of the Liverpool bards. They had also clashed with the famously severe poetry critic Ian Hamilton, and with the *Times Literary Supplement*, a refusal of endorsement that probably did their image no harm. At its best this poetry was witty and fun, at its worst a blend of art-school pretension and pop banality: Batman rubbing shoulders with Père Ubu. I found Adrian Henri the most interesting of the three. A graduate of Fine Arts from Durham University (though naturally enough we only heard about the career in a North Wales fairground), Henri was a fine artist (his work is in the Walker Art Gallery) who won the John Moores prize in 1972 and had an exhibition at the ICA in 1968. Like McGough he formed a poetry/rock group, Liverpool Scene, and he was the most literary of the group. Willett again:

> His special contribution has been to sense the relevance of [Dada/avant-garde movements] and other apparently rarefied manifestations of the modern movement to the particular climate of Liverpool, for which he has great feeling and affection... As a poet he has been able to put the key figures in his mythology, from T. S. Eliot to the film *Ashes and Diamonds* into a Liverpool context and make them seem at home there; it was he, for instance, who organised a Père Ubu procession to Falkner Square on Alfred Jarry's ninety-first birthday.

I knew one of the Liverpool poets who described a plan (which as far as I know never came to fruition) to scatter white flowers all around the boundary of Liverpool 8 on a particular day. Liverpool 8 was the district near the University and the

Anglican cathedral where many of the poets lived, as often as not, in rented rooms in faded yet elegant Georgian terraces. There was something touching about the wish to beautify it in the imagination.

One of the leading metropolitan advocates of the Liverpool poets was Edward Lucie-Smith, whose anthology *The Liverpool Scene* appeared in the same year as the best-selling Penguin Modern Poets No. 10. He put his finger on the mixture of provincial-metropolitan dialectic, the purely Scouse elements, and the powerful sense of place in this movement:

> To the outsider, the city [in 1967] has a strangely derelict air. There are many stretches of featureless rubble, many broken windows, many buildings in bad repair... But the city continues to think of itself as something pretty special... Its inhabitants are gifted with a famous sarcasm... the success of the Beatles had a seismic effect on the provincial culture as a whole. For the first time London has been left out in the cold till the very last minute... poetry in Liverpool is more uninhibitedly colourful, more deliberately 'public' than at any other place in the British Isles.

Lucie-Smith even claimed that 'the traditional brutality of Liverpool humour is especially close to Jarry'. He maintained that there had never been a time when young poets in the provinces had been so 'bored and impatient with the work held up to them as an example by the reviewers in London'. The problem with this line of argument, however attractive, and however much one would like to believe it, is that it has not proved workable given the centralising trends of contemporary culture – particularly in publishing and bookselling – which have accelerated at an alarming rate since the 1960s. Lucie-Smith was actually one of those 'reviewers in London' and both the key anthologies came from London publishers. The Beatles were published by EMI. Provincial culture – if that

170

is what it is and if the term has any meaning – still depends on metropolitan mediation and validation. The old monopolies have not been knocked off their perches. And they don't look like being.

But, yes, the poems were fun. Like Adrian Henri's short 'Liverpool Poems':

> Prostitutes in the snow in Canning St like strange erotic
> snowmen
> And Marcel Proust in the Kardomah eating Madeleine
> butties dipped in tea.

There were other Liverpool poets, too, like Matt Simpson, who didn't have the same media exposure. In a recent anthology called *Liverpool Accents* (1996), which contains the work of seven poets who have had some connection with the city, or who, like Simpson, were born there, the poets were invited to comment. Simpson makes some very shrewd observations about Liverpool humour:

> But beneath the toughness and the satirical edge can often
> be perceived a soft-heartedness, a generosity, which can
> teeter on and sometimes totter over the edge of sentimen-
> tality. A lot of the abrasiveness of recent Liverpool writing
> is simply an inverted sentimentality. A couple of pints and
> we're anybody's.

Guilty as charged.

Coda

It is a July evening on the Pier Head at Liverpool and I am sitting on a sunny bench facing the River Mersey. I am also facing a memorial to men of the merchant navy who lost their lives in the Second World War and who – as the chiselled lettering reads – 'gave their lives willingly for the freedom of others and have no grave but the sea'.

I am struck by the effectiveness of simple words.

No grave but the sea.

It has been a long day. For nine hours I have tramped the streets of my native city, looking, listening, remembering, trying to see old things in a new light, seeeing, frankly, things from time to time that I had never seen before. Like a social anthropologist, I suppose, one needs to be able to stand back, to acquire, in that happy phrase of Claude Lévi-Strauss, *le regard lointain.* A bit of perspective helps.

The most ardent patriots are the absentee patriots and I am one of these now. I must shortly catch my train home. I left Liverpool in the summer of 1973, unaware that I was part of a trend, a flight from the city which, say the statistics,

172

is now reversed. The city is on the up-and-up. They are selling a lot of lofts.

I have already made too many references to the European Capital of Culture status. Liverpool's riverfront is also a UNESCO World Heritage Site. I hope these accolades will mean something more than tourist cliché and marketing-speak. I hope they will mark the city's confirmation of revival, after those rather difficult years at the end of the twentieth century.

On my long day as a Liverpool *flâneur* I called in around lunchtime, as I passed through Exchange Flags, at Philpott's the sandwich bar. If you are in Liverpool and want a great sandwich there is simply nowhere else to go. Sandwiches are made to order in front of you on a marble slab and if this were London it would be characterised by a certain hauteur and self-importance, but the sandwich-makers here are nothing if not down to earth. Tempted by the possibility of avocado, chicken and bacon, I was asked, when my turn came at the slab, if I wanted butter or olive oil. I can't think of anywhere else in Liverpool where such a question would be put. 'I've never 'ad avocado,' the woman said with a lively, friendly smile as she chopped and sliced. 'But they say it's supposed to be very nice.'

It was, luv. It was.

That note of cheerful realism – a very Liverpudlian note – was struck again when I called in a little later at the splendid News from Nowhere radical bookshop in Bold Street. I was nosing around in the miscellaneous pamphlets and books on local history and when I came to pay I noticed some more local history books on a shelf behind the till. 'I see you've got some more up there,' I said. The bookseller urged me to have a look, explaining why they were nearly out of reach: 'They tend to get nicked.' Recounting this story to a Liverpudlian friend I was soundly rebuked for 'stereotyping', for adding to the stock of bad old images of Liverpool. Perhaps the criticism was just but at the same time the story was true (and I have suppressed another, more damning, that had occurred in my sight fifteen minutes beforehand). And Liverpool – which is far from being a den of thieves – I like to think retains the gift of being able to laugh at itself.

On my sunny bench, I watched the relaxed strolling up and down of the Liverpudlians taking the evening air. A man with a push-bike. Some Japanese tourists endlessly photographing each other. A young man with his nose deep in a book, suddenly disturbed by the Japanese who wanted him to take a group photograph with the Mersey as backdrop. For thirty years I had been away, returning regularly to visit family. I had fallen in love here. This place was a part of me, *is* a part of me, yet, like so many others, I do not live here. Three decades ago I thought only of getting the hell out of it, as young men invariably do. As a teenager I was a fanatical Joycean, *A Portrait of the Artist as a Young Man* was my sacred text. The ardent wish of Stephen Dedalus to fly past the nets of everything that tied him to one particular place and its demanding history was mine too. I thought only of escape. But I ended up in London, not Trieste. Joyce never got Dublin out of his system and didn't want to. I am not Joyce but my native city is in my blood also, whether I wish it to be or not.

Liverpool is, above all, a seaport, with comings and goings, provisional encounters, long absences, farewells and greetings, inscribed in its essential character. Like everyone else I will keep on coming back.

Liverpool is also a provincial city. The adjective is often used pejoratively, as if it implies a settling for the second rate, an *ersatz* metropolis. In certain countries of Europe this would not be the case. In these a 'provincial' newspaper or publishing house is as good as a national one. British culture is still too centred on London for that to be the case and it is hard for the provinces to fight back, to mark out their own space. But it is a fight worth picking. Cities such as Liverpool preserve something vital in an increasingly homogenised, centralised culture that appears to put less and less value on diversity and difference, appears indeed to be increasingly indifferent if not hostile to such things. The insistence – the natural, instinctive reflex – in Liverpool that things should be done differently, that one should be defiant and cheeky, speak 'with an accent exceedingly rare', pluck down pretension, refuse to take the metropolis at its own valuation, is its great, invincible strength.

Liverpool has always gone its own way. It always will.

Bibliography

Ackah, William, and Mark Christian (eds.), *Black Organisation and Identity in Liverpool: A Local, National and Global Perspective*, 1997

Aiken, John, *A Description of the Country from Thirty to Forty Miles Round Manchester*, 1795

Allen, Sarah, *My Liverpool Home*, 1979

'An Old Stager', *Liverpool A Few Years Since*, 3rd edn, 1885

Anon., *The Picture of Liverpool or Stranger's Guide*, 1805

Anon., *A General and Descriptive History of the Ancient and Present State of the Town of Liverpool*, 1795

Anon., *The Liverpool Irishman or Annals of the Irish*, 2nd edn, 1924

Anon., *Liverpool and Slavery: An Historical Account of the Liverpool–African Slave Trade, by a Genuine 'Dicky Sam'*, 1884

Anon., *Liverpool, a Satire*, 1808

Armstrong, Rev. R. A., 'The Call of God to the Middle Classes of England', from *The Liverpool Pulpit*, Vol. 1 No. 5, June 1892

Askey, Arthur, *Before Your Very Eyes*, 1975

Ayers, Pat, *The Liverpool Docklands: Life and Work in Athol Street*, 1989

Bainbridge, Beryl, *Harriet Said...*, 1972

Baines, Thomas, *Liverpool in 1859*, 1859

Bell, S. B. (ed.), *Victorian Lancashire*, 1974

Birrell, Augustine, *Some Early Recollections of Liverpool*, 1924

Bleasdale, Alan, *Boys from the Blackstuff*, ed. David Self, 1985

Boney, Knowles, *Liverpool Porcelain of the Eighteenth Century and its*

Makers, 1957

Bowker, Gordon, *Pursued by Furies: A Life of Malcolm Lowry*, 1993

Box, Charles, *Liverpool Overhead Railway 1893–1956*, 1959

Braddock, Jack, and Bessie Braddock, *The Braddocks*, 1963

Briggs, Asa, *Friends of the People: The Centenary History of Lewis's*, 1956

Briscoe, Diana, *Wicked Scouse English*, 2003

Brooke, Richard, *Liverpool as it was During the Last Quarter of the Eighteenth Century, 1775–1800*, 1853

Brown, Hugh Stowell, *Twelve Lectures to the Men of Liverpool, Lecture VIII, The Street*, 1858

Burgess, Anthony, *Byrne*, 1995

Caine, W. S. (ed.), *Hugh Stowell Brown: His Autobiography*, 1887

Camden, William, *Britannia*, 1586

Cameron, Gail, and Stan Cooke, *Liverpool – Capital of the Slave Trade*, 1992

Čapek, Karel, *Letters from England*, 1924, trans. Geoffrey Newsome, 2001

Chandler, George, *William Roscoe of Liverpool*, 1953

Cockcroft, William, 'The Liverpool Police Force, 1836–1902', in Bell (ed.), *Victorian Lancashire*

Coles, Gladys Mary, *Both Sides of the River: Merseyside in Poetry and Prose*, 1993

Conor, John A., *The Struggles of an Infant Parish*, 1854

Costello, Ray, *Black Liverpool: The Early History of Britain's Oldest Black Community 1730–1918*, 2001

Cropper, James, *On the Injurious Effects of High Prices of Produce, and the Beneficial Effects of Low Prices on the Condition of Slaves: A Letter Addressed to the Liverpool Society for Promoting the Abolition of Slavery*, 1823

Davis, Merrell R., and William H. Gilman, *The Letters of Herman Melville*, 1960

Davies, Terence, *A Modest Pageant*, 1992

Davies, Terence, *Hallelujah Now*, 1984

Dawson, Jerry, *Left Theatre: Merseyside Unity Theatre: A Documentary Record*, 1985

De La Salle, the Venerable, *The Rules of Christian Politeness*, trans. from the French by Mrs J. Sadlier, 1862

Defoe, Daniel, *A Tour Through the Whole Island of Great Britain: Vol. 3 Letter IV, Containing a Description of the Counties of Lancaster*,

Westmorland, and Cumberland, 1721–6, 1727
Denvir, John, *The Life Story of an Old Rebel*, 1910
Dickens, Charles, *The Uncommercial Traveller*, 1860
Duncan, Dr William H., *The Sessional Papers of the House of Lords XXIV, App, 14-25*, 1844
Enfield, William, *An Essay Towards the History of Leverpool drawn up by the papers left by the late Mr George Perry and from other papers left by William Enfield*, 1773
Finch, John, *Statistics of Vauxhall Ward, Liverpool*, 1842 (reproduced in facsimile with an introduction by Harold Hikins, 1986)
Fordham, John, *James Hanley: Modernism and the Working Class*, 2002
Forwood, William B., *Recollections of a Busy Life: Being the Reminiscences of a Liverpool Merchant 1840–1910*, 1910
Galbraith, Georgina (ed.), *The Journal of the Rev. William Bagshaw Stevens*, 1965
Gladstone, William, *Autobiography*, 1880
Glasgow, Eric, *The Making of Victorian Southport*, 2000
Grace, Sherrill E. (ed.), *The Collected Letters of Malcolm Lowry, Volume 1: 1926–1946*, 1995
Hanley, James, *Herman Melville: A Man in the Custom House*, 1971
— *Summary-Report of the Police Proceedings* (summary in British Library of a report in the *Manchester Guardian* of 21st March 1935), 1935
— *Broken Water: An Autobiographical Excursion*, 1937
— *The Ocean*, 1941
— *The Last Voyage and Other Stories*, 1997 [1931]
Hawthorne, Nathaniel, *The English Notebooks*, ed. Randall Stewart, 1941, Boston
Hignett, Sean, *A Picture to Hang on the Wall*, 1966
Hikins, Harold R. (ed.), *Building the Union: Studies on the Growth of the Workers' Movement*, 1973
Hocking, Silas, *Her Benny*, 1879
Hopkins, Gerard Manley, *Letters to Robert Bridges*, ed. Claude Colleer Abbott, 1935; *Further Letters of Gerard Manley Hopkins*, 1956 (first edn 1938)
— *The Journals and Papers of Gerard Manley Hopkins*, ed. Humphry House, 1959
Hopkinson, J., *Memoirs of a Victorian Cabinet Maker*, ed. J. B. Goodman, 1968

Hughes, Quentin, *Seaport*, 1964

Hume, A., *The Condition of Liverpool: Religious and Social*, 2nd edn, 1858

Hunter, Bill, *Forgotten Hero: The Life and Times of Edward Rushton*, 2002

John, Augustus, *Chiaroscuro: Fragments of Autobiography*, 1952

Jones, Jack, *Union Man*, 1986

Jones, R. Merfyn, and D. Ben Rees, *Liverpool Welsh and their Religion*, 1984

Jung, Carl Gustav, *Memories, Dreams, Reflections*, 1963

Kazantzakis, Nikos, *England: A Travel Journal*, 1965

Kenny, Anthony, *A Path From Rome*, 1986

Kilvert, Francis, *Kilvert's Diary: Selections from the Diary of the Reverend Francis Kilvert*, ed. William Plomer, 1938; corrected 1961

Lancaster, H. Boswell, *Liverpool and her Potters*, 1936

Lane, Tony, *Liverpool: Gateway of Empire*, 1987 (second edition published as *Liverpool: City of the Sea*, 1997)

Leland, John, *Itinerary*, 1533–39 (cited in Lucie-Smith, *The Liverpool Scene*, 'Introduction')

Leyda, Jay, *The Melville Log: A Documentary Life of Herman Melville 1819–91*, 2nd edn, 1969

Liddell, Robert, *Cavafy: A Biography*, 1974

Lindop, Grevel, *The Opium-Eater: A Life of Thomas de Quincey*, 1981

Lucie-Smith, Edward (ed.), *The Liverpool Scene*, 1967

Macnaughton, Donald A., *Roscoe of Liverpool, His Life, Writings and Treasures*, 1996

Mann, Tom, *Memoirs*, 1923

Marriner, S., *The Economic and Social Development of Merseyside*, 1982

Masefield, John, *The Conway*, 1933; revised edn, 1953

Mellow, James R., *Nathaniel Hawthorne in His Times*, Boston, 1980

Melly, George, *Liverpool, Stray Leaves*, n.d.

Melville, Herman, *Redburn: His First Voyage*, 1849, ed. with an intro by Harold Beaver, 1976

Merseyside Community Relations Council, *Racial Discrimination and Disadvantage in Employment in Liverpool: Evidence submitted to the House of Commons Select Committee on Employment by MCRC and Liverpool Black Caucus, in association with Merseyside Area Profile Group, Department of Sociology, University of Liverpool. February 1986*, 1986

Midwinter, Eric, *Old Liverpool*, 1971

Miller, Edwin Haviland, *Salem is My Dwelling Place: A Life of Hawthorne*, 1991

Morris, Christopher (ed.), *The Journeys of Celia Fiennes*, 1949

Murphy, Michael (ed.), *The Collected George Garrett*, 1999

Murray, Nicholas, 'Three Versions of Liverpool' in *Plausible Fictions*, 1995 (reprinted in *The Narrators*, 2006)

— *A Life of Matthew Arnold*, 1996

— *A Short Book About Love*, 2001

Neal, F., *Sectarian Violence: The Liverpool Experience, 1819–1914*, 1988

O'Connor, Thomas, *Tom O'Connor's Book of Liverpool Humour*, 1987

O'Mara, Pat, *The Autobiography of a Liverpool Slummy*, 1934

Olmsted, Frederick Law, *Walks and Talks of an American Farmer in England*, 1859

Orwell, Sonia, and Ian Angus (eds), *The Collected Essays, Journalism and Letters of George Orwell, Volume 1, An Age Like This, 1920–1940*, 1965

Parker, Hershel, *Herman Melville: A Biography, Volume 1, 1819–1851*, 1996

Phillips, Catherine (ed.), *Gerard Manley Hopkins: Selected Letters*, 1991

Picton, J. A., *Memorials of Liverpool: Historical and Topgraphical*, 2nd edn, revised, 1907

Quincey, Thomas de, *The Confessions of an English Opium Eater*, 1821

Read, Brian Ahier, *Vanished Liverpool and the San'tree Man: Recollections of a Sanitary Inspector in Scotland Road 50 Years Ago*, 2001

Rees, D. Ben, *The Welsh of Merseyside, Vol. 1*, 1997

Roberts, Eleazar, *Owen Rees: A Story of Welsh Life and Thought*, 1893

Samuelson, James, *The Children of Our Slums*, 1911

Sassoon, Siegfried, *Memories of an Infantry Officer*, 1930

Sellers, Ian, *Nineteenth Century Liverpool and the Novelists*, 1979

Shaw, Frank, *Lern Yerself Scouse* ed. Fritz Spiegl, 1966

Shimmin, Hugh, *Liverpool Life*, 1857

Simey, Margaret, *Charitable Effort in Liverpool in the Nineteenth Century*, 1951

Smithers, Henry, *Liverpool, its Commerce, Statistics, and Institutions with a History of the Cotton Trade*, 1825

Southey, Robert, *Letters from England*, ed. Jack Simmons, 1984

Stonehouse, James, *The Stranger in Liverpool or An Historical and Descriptive View of Liverpool and its Environs, 1807*, reprinted by Liverpool Libraries Department, 2002

Stonehouse, James, *The Streets of Liverpool*, 1869

Stonor, Robert Julian, *Liverpool's Hidden Story*, 1957

Taine, Hippolyte, *Notes on England* (*Notes sur l'Angleterre*), 1873, trans. Edward Hyams, 1995

Thomas, Mark, *Every Mother's Nightmare: The Killing of James Bulger*, 1993

Tocqueville, Alexis de, *Journey to England*, 1835; trans. George Lawrence and K. P. Mayer, 1958

Toole, Millie, *Mrs Bessie Braddock MP: A Biography*, 1957

Troughton, Thomas, *The History of Liverpool, from the Earliest, Authenticated Period down to the Present Time*, 1810

Wah, Yung Yung, Burjor Avari and Simon Buckley, *British Soil Chinese Roots: Chinese Life in Britain*, 1996

Waller, P. J., *Democracy and Sectarianism: A Political and Social History of Liverpool 1868–1939*, 1981

Walton, John K., and Alastair Wilcox (eds), *Low Life and Improvement in Mid-Victorian England: Liverpool through the Journalism of Hugh Shimmin*, 1991

White, B. D., *A History of the Corporation of Liverpool*, 1951

Wilkinson, Colin, *The Streets of Liverpool*, 1993

Willett, John, *Art in a City*, 1967 (republished with an introduction by Bryan Biggs, 2007)

Wilson, Jean Moorcroft, *Siegfried Sassoon: The Making of a War Poet. A Biography (1886–1918)*, 1998

Winskill, P. T., and J. Thomas, *History of the Temperance Movement in Liverpool and District*, 1887

Wong, Maria Lin, *Chinese Liverpudlians: A History of the Chinese Community in Liverpool*, 1989

Woodson, Thomas, and Bill Ellis, *Nathaniel Hawthorne: The English Notebooks, Vol. 1 1853–56; Vol. 2 1856–60*, 1997

Woolf, Virginia, *A Passionate Apprentice – The Early Journals*, ed. Mitchell A. Leaska, 1990

Worpole, Ken, *Dockers and Detectives: Popular Reading, Popular Writing*, 1983

Wyn Davies, David, *Owen Owen: Victorian Draper*, 1984